Strength and Dignity

Torah Wisdom for Women
on their
Multitude of Vital Roles

Writings of the Lubavitcher Rebbe,
Compiled, translated, and introduced
By
Dr. Naomi Zirkind

STRENGTH AND DIGNITY

First Edition 5771-2011
Second Revised Edition 5773-2013

ISBN 978-1481933193

Table of Contents

Table of Contents 3

Acknowledgements 7

Notes on the Translation 8

Endorsements 9

Preface 11

Parashat Bereishit 17
The importance of an enthusiasm for observance of the
commandments

Parashat Noach 21
Influencing the world in a pleasant way

Parashat Lech Lecha 27
A man's wealth is earned through the merit of his wife

Parashat Vayeira 33
Bringing up one's children according to the highest standard

Parashat Chayei Sarah 37
Serving God with all of one's abilities

Parashat Toldot 43
A wife's influence on her husband

Parashat Vayeitzei 45
The far-reaching effects of how a mother raises her children

Parashat Vayishlach 47
Exerting a positive influence on other Jewish women

Parashat Vayeishev 55
Serving God with self-sacrifice

4

Parashat Mikeitz 61
Illuminating the home with Torah even when there are
difficulties

Parashat Vayigash 65
Transforming the physical world to make it display God's
presence

Parashat Vayechi 71
Giving up one's own spiritual benefit for the sake of one's
children

Parashat Shemot 77
The heroic Jewish women in Egypt set an example for us

Parashat Va'eira 81
The merit of the women brings the redemption

Parashat Bo 85
Education of Jewish children

Parashat Beshalach 89
A mother's joy at the rescue of her children

Parashat Yitro 101
The women were first at the giving of the Torah

Parashat Mishpatim 105
The Shabbat candles bring light to the whole family

Parashat Terumah 109
Making one's home a dwelling place for God

Parashat Tetzaveh 111
Beautifying one's surroundings for God

Parashat Ki Tisa 115
Women's special ability to express faith through action

Parashat Vayakhel 121
Women's enthusiasm for making a dwelling place for God

Parashat Pekudei 125
Bringing holiness into the desert

Parashat Vayikra 129
Doing the mitzvot in the most beautiful way possible

Parashat Tzav 133
  The Holy Temple service benefits the entire Jewish nation

Parashat Shemini.. 137
  The vital importance of the observance of kashrut

Parashat Tazria 143
  The power of Shabbat candles to overcome impurity

Parashat Metzora 151
  The vital importance of the observance of the laws of family
  purity

Parashat Acharei Mot... 155
  Synthesis of the spiritual and the physical

Parashat Kedoshim... 159
  Love for one's fellow Jew

Parashat Emor 161
  How women should relate to the outside world

Parashat Behar... 167
  Bringing holiness into everyday activities

Parashat Bechukotai 171
  Modest conduct brings great blessings

Parashat Bamidbar... 175
  Raising a generation of children for God's army

Parashat Naso.. 179
  Hair covering for married women

Parashat Beha'alotecha... 183
  Lighting up the world

Parashat Shlach 187
  The love of women for the Land of Israel – physical and spiritual

Parashat Korach 191
  The tremendous influence of the wife

Parashat Chukat... 195
  Making Torah accessible to even the youngest

Parashat Balak 201
  Diligent observance of the principles of modest conduct

Parashat Pinchas 205
 Happy is the person whose words God acknowledges

Parashat Matot.. 209
 The tremendous value of serving God through involvement
 with the physical world

Parashat Mas'ei 215
 Trust in God when seeking a spouse

Parashat Devarim.. 219
 Transforming the material world into a Godly place

Parashat Vaetchanan 223
 Mezuzot protect the Jewish home

Parashat Eikev 227
 Making God's presence perceptible in all aspects of life

Parashat Re'ei 231
 The special quality of a woman's charity

Parashat Shoftim 235
 Sensitivity to holiness

Parashat Ki Teitzei 239
 Modest conduct brings God's protection

Parashat Ki Tavo 243
 Being happy brings blessings

Parashat Nitzavim 247
 Observance of the commandments even in a foreign land

Parashat Vayeilech.. 251
 Assembling one's personal capabilities for the service of God

Parashat Ha'azinu... 253
 Fostering the proper attitude toward material wealth

Parashat Vezot Habracha.. 257
 Education of young children

Appendix.. 261

Glossary.. 263

Index 267

Acknowledgements

First, I thank God for giving me life, health, strength, and all the other resources necessary to complete the composition of this book. It has taken me over nine years, and I have faced many obstacles to completion of the book, but God has helped me to persevere and to overcome them. Thank God for His infinite kindness.

Thanks to my mother, Rebbetzin Rachael Silman, for all her encouragement and support throughout the years of effort to get the book written and published.

Thanks to my husband, Rabbi Yaakov Mendel Zirkind, for all of his support for my writing the book, and for his continued encouragement.

My talented editors, Rabbi Shmuel Klatzkin and Kayla Klatzkin, have greatly improved the clarity and conciseness of the manuscript. Mark Levin and Malka Weintraub edited the manuscript to improve its clarity. Rabbi Zalman Dubinsky edited the manuscript for accuracy. Avrohom Weg designed the book cover. Yosef Yitzchok Turner formatted the interior text.

All citations of verses from the Artscroll Tanach were reproduced from the Artscroll Stone Edition "Tanach" with permission from the copyright holders, Artscroll / Mesorah Publications, Ltd.

6 Elul 5771
Morristown, New Jersey

לעילוי נשמת אבי מורי

הרב משה דובער ז״ל בן הרב יעקב אליעזר ז״ל סילמאן

Notes on the Translation

The original texts of the Rebbe's writings are in various volumes of "Likkutei Sichos" or "Sefer Hasichos", published by Kehot Publication Society, 770 Eastern Parkway, Brooklyn, NY 11213.

Untranslated words in this text are italicized and are defined in the Glossary at the end of the book. In the Lubavitcher Rebbe's original writings, italics were used for emphasis; however, these words are underlined in this book in order to distinguish the emphasized words from the Glossary words.

Some explanatory notes and footnotes were inserted by the author into the translated texts. These notes are enclosed in square brackets ("[ ]").

The author is responsible for any errors in translation.

Endorsements

זלמן דובינסקי ר"י ישיבת תפארת בחורים מוריסטאון נו דשערסי
Rabbi Zalman Dubinsky
Rosh Yeshiva, Yeshivas Tiferes Bachurim
Morristown, N.J. 07960

After examining the manuscript "Strength and Dignity" by Dr. Naomi Zirkind, I highly recommend this scholarly work for both laymen and scholar, for women and for men too.

The goal of manuscript is -as Dr. Naomi Zirkind mentions in the introduction - "to present a selection of the Rebbe's writings on the special roles of Jewish women. This topic was very important to the Rebbe, and he devoted many discourses and letters to it. He emphasized the critical importance of women's various roles to the integrity of Jewish life".

"Strength and Dignity" is an extremely valuable tool that can and should be used in various formats to inspire the wife and mother, as well as the future wives and mothers in their unique role of being the "*akeres habayis*"-the base and foundation of the Jewish home.

In our day and age when Jewish education in general and especially the Jewish education of girls has become more challenging than perhaps ever before, in a time when the darkness of the outside world has managed to cover and hide the innocence and purity of our children, we must counteract this with additional light and holiness. One of the most powerful tools for doing this is using the Shabbat meals to show and explain to our children the value and treasure of our identity, and to teach and guide them to appreciate our G-d given mission, with clarity as to our goals and how to achieve them. I would strongly suggest that "Strength and Dignity" should be used at the Shabbat table for this purpose. And yes, men too will greatly benefit from this.

I would suggest that "Strength and Dignity should be used in our Schools as a text book for their studies. It should be emphasized that this is an excellent tool to be used by parents in preparing their daughter for Bat Mitzvah.

It is clear that this book is an important part of the process of spreading the wellsprings of Chassidut outward, and it hastens the coming of Mashiach, may it happen immediately.

וברור שספר זה הרי זה חלק חשוב בהפצת המעיינות חוצה, שעל ידי זה ממהרים ביאת המשיח תיכף ומיד ממש.

[signature]

ב״ה

22 Elul 5770
September 1, 2010

Dr. Naomi Zirkind
374 Sussex Avenue
Morristown, NJ 07960

Dear Dr. Zirkind: נ״י

My wife Rebbetzin Mindel Feiler and I are deeply impressed and inspired with your scholarly work, "Strength and Dignity," talks from the Rebbe relating to women from each of the weekly Torah readings. This was a project "begging" to be done, and you have the eternal merit of "making it happen."

May this zchus of spreading the Rebbe's instructions evoke for you and your family God's blessings for the fulfillment of your hearts' desires for all good.

Kesiva Vachasima Tova,

Rabbi Moshe Feller

Preface

Any complex appliance comes with a user's manual written by the manufacturer. This manual tells the user detailed information about the appliance, such as how to activate its various functions and how to maintain it. Someone who would purchase a complex appliance without receiving the manual would have great difficulty trying to figure out how to use it. Thus, it would seem very peculiar if a human being, who is more complex than any appliance, would come without a user's manual written by his "manufacturer."

In fact, God, the manufacturer of mankind and everything in the universe, has provided a user's manual for the human race. Although manmade user's manuals can sometimes be intimidating or "user-unfriendly," the manual written by God is perfectly designed and easily accessible. This manual is called Torah, a name related to the Hebrew word *hora'ah*, meaning teaching. The Torah teaches the way to conduct oneself in order to effectively utilize all of one's capabilities. Although the Torah mainly discusses the life of a Jew, it also presents the seven commandments that apply to all humanity, so that every person may learn from it how to lead a meaningful and productive life.

Since God gave the Torah a few thousand years ago, Jews have faithfully followed its teachings. However, the level of people's spiritual sensitivity has generally diminished from one generation to the next. In the past several hundred years, it has become necessary for deeper levels of the Torah to become revealed to compensate for this diminution and to maintain the Jews' living connection with God.

A parable[1] will make this phenomenon easier to understand. A king's son was very sick. No cure could be found for his illness and he became sicker and sicker, to the point that he could not even eat or drink any medicine that might be given to him. Finally, a doctor was found who knew what would cure the prince. This doctor said that the only thing that would work would be to remove the most precious jewel from the king's crown, grind it up into a powder, mix it with water, and give the mixture to the prince to drink. The king agreed to do whatever was necessary to save his son and had the mixture prepared. The prince was too sick to drink; only a few drops somehow made it down his throat. But even this small amount of medicine was enough to help the prince recover.

In this analogy the king represents God, the prince represents the Jewish nation, and the illness represents the deterioration in spiritual sensitivity all too common in our society. The cure, the crown jewel, symbolizes the deepest levels of the Torah, levels that had hitherto been hidden and understood by only a select few. The teachings of *Chassidut* provide this spiritual cure, they elucidate the inner dimensions of Torah in a way that can be understood by all Jews, each one according to his/her spiritual and intellectual level.

In the present generation, the Lubavitcher Rebbe, Rabbi Menachem Mendel Schneerson (may his merit protect us; henceforth referred to as "the Rebbe"), expressed the teachings of *Chassidut* in a way that is accessible. He has spread these teachings to Jews around the world, through his emissaries, to an unprecedented extent. Through his influence, he transformed the entire landscape of Jewish life and brought countless individuals to higher levels of Torah observance and closeness to God.

---

1   This parable was composed by Rabbi Schneur Zalman of Liadi, the founder and first Rebbe of Chabad/Lubavitch Chassidism.

The Rebbe left hundreds of discourses and letters, which range in subject matter from esoteric analyses of topics in Torah to everyday guidance. However lofty the subject matter, he emphasized how it should be implemented in our lives. By teaching us how to apply the inner dimensions of the Torah in a practical way, he gave us the "medicine" that we need in order to be spiritually healthy. Once the spiritual aspects of life are in order, all other aspects fall into place as well.

The goal of this book is to present a selection of the Rebbe's writings on the special roles of Jewish women. This topic was very important to the Rebbe and he devoted many discourses and letters to it. He emphasized the critical importance of women's various roles for ensuring the integrity of Jewish life.

Each chapter is devoted to one of the weekly Torah portions and features an excerpt from the Rebbe's writings about women. The chapter begins with an introduction that explains a topic from the Torah portion and how the excerpt from the Rebbe's writings relates to that topic. Then, an English translation of the excerpt is presented, with a citation for those who wish to read the entire discourse or letter. This chapter structure allows for study of the material at various levels of depth. For the reader's convenience, the book includes an Appendix with a table that shows the chapter and verse with which each *parsha* begins and ends.

The updated version of this book includes a study guide which consists of a set of review questions at the end of each chapter. The purpose of this study guide is to facilitate the use of the book in a classroom setting or in a group discussion setting. The review questions lead the reader through the train of thought in the excerpt from the Rebbe's writings. The answers to all the questions are found in the excerpt – no outside sources are required in order to find answers to them.

The sets of questions could be used in a variety of ways, depending on the type of student to which the material is being presented, for example:

- For younger students without much background knowledge of *Chassidut*, the questions could be used as an outline for the teacher's lesson plan, and the teacher could present the material in her own words based on this outline.

- For more mature students without much background knowledge of *Chassidut*, the questions can be used as a framework for a preparatory discussion, after which the actual text of the chapter could be studied.

- For students with substantial background knowledge of *Chassidut*, the questions could be used as a homework assignment for the students to deepen their understanding of the material.

- An individual reader can use the questions to check her understanding of the material.

* * *

King Solomon, the wisest of all people, wrote a poem[2] that describes the special virtues of the Jewish woman. In this poem, one phrase seems to encompass the other virtues: "*Oz vehadar levushah*,"[3] which can be translated as "Strength and dignity are her garb."[4] The title of this book – *Strength and Dignity* – is borrowed from that phrase, since it is about the special powers of character that God invests in the Jewish woman and about her responsibility to actualize these qualities through her actions.

The Rebbe's writings on the role of Jewish women are permeated with the underlying themes of strength and

---

2   Proverbs 31
3   Proverbs 31:25
4   *Siddur Tehillat Hashem with English Translation, Annotated Edition*, Merkos L'Inyonei Chinuch, Brooklyn, NY, 2002; page 177.

dignity. One of the main themes that appears in these writings is the fact that the woman is the *akeret habayit* (spiritual foundation of the home). In this role, she sets the tone for the spiritual atmosphere in her household. For this role, she needs a great deal of strength to maintain the proper atmosphere in all circumstances. Another theme is that the woman's manner of influence on others is one of pleasantness and warmth. The regal bearing that is manifested by this approach can be described by the word *hadar*, which can be translated as dignity, glory, or splendor

* * *

A description of the events that led to the composition of this book would help elucidate its value and utility. As my oldest daughter approached the age of Bat Mitzvah, I wanted to find a way to help her prepare for this momentous event. My oldest son had recently celebrated his Bar Mitzvah and had prepared for it extensively by learning and memorizing lengthy sections of Chassidic writings and by composing a discussion of an aspect of the laws of *tefillin*. 'How,' I wondered, 'could I give my daughter a preparation this meaningful that would be appropriate for a girl?'

I decided to study a selection from the Rebbe's writings about women with her once a week. How should I go about selecting a text to study? The first Lubavitcher Rebbe, Rabbi Schneur Zalman of Liadi, had a saying that one must "live with the time." This saying has been explained in Chassidic writings[5] to mean that at any given time, one should seek guidance from the weekly Torah portion. Therefore, each week, I endeavored to find a text about one of the roles of women, which would relate to a topic in the Torah portion for that week.

---

5   Rabbi Menachem M. Schneerson, *Hayom Yom*, Kehot Publication Society, Brooklyn, New York, 1943; section for 2 Cheshvan.

In the process of working on this project, I began to feel the immense value of this collection of the Rebbe's writing. It has been a helpful guide for me in a variety of situations throughout my life. Since the chapters are related to the Torah portions, it is also a source of weekly inspiration. Because these teachings are so precious, I have worked hard to transform them into a book that could be useful to all Jewish women.

The texts presented in *Strength and Dignity* cover an array of topics that relate to many areas of life and thus will be useful to a wide variety of women. They can also be used to help prepare a girl for her Bat Mitzvah, as I had originally done. A noteworthy feature of the Rebbe's writings is his focus on the special value of children. Although they do not yet fulfill the adult roles that are discussed so extensively, the Rebbe often points out the importance of the fact that they are in the process of preparing for these roles. Thus, through this book, children – and pre-Bat Mitzvah girls in particular– can feel that they, too, are doing something important in their lives. Furthermore, *Strength and Dignity* will be useful for any Jewish woman who would like to better understand the special value of her varied roles and to receive guidance on the best way to fulfill them.

I hope that the reader will find *Strength and Dignity* to be a helpful guide and a source of encouragement, and that the accompanying study guide will be a helpful tool for teaching the material to students. It was in the merit of the righteous women that the Jews were redeemed from exile in Egypt long ago. So too, the merits of the women of our generation will bring the final and complete redemption that we are all waiting for. I hope the publication of *Strength and Dignity* will increase the merits of women today, and thus hasten the redemption – may it materialize speedily in our days!

Parashat Bereishit

THE IMPORTANCE OF AN ENTHUSIASM
FOR OBSERVANCE OF THE COMMANDMENTS

Parashat Bereishit describes God's creation of the world. After He created Adam, He placed Adam in the Garden of Eden and told him that he may eat from any tree in the garden except for the Tree of Knowledge. After giving this command to Adam, God created Eve to be a wife for him. Eve heard the command about the Tree of Knowledge only indirectly, from Adam. One of the creatures in the garden, the snake, approached Eve and enticed her to eat some fruit from the Tree of Knowledge. Eve enjoyed the fruit and convinced Adam to eat some of it as well. God punished Adam and Eve and all of their descendants – the entirety of humanity – for their transgression.

In the following excerpt from a discourse, the Rebbe mentions the statement of our Sages that when God gave the Torah to the Jews, He first spoke to the women and then to the men, in order to prevent any mishap such as that which occurred in the Garden of Eden. The Rebbe explains that if Eve had heard the command directly from God, she would not only have refused to eat the fruit, she would also have prevented her husband from eating it. Thus, we learn the vital importance of a woman's enthusiasm for the observance of *mitzvot*, an enthusiasm of the type that would come from hearing the commandment directly from God. If she does have such an enthusiasm, she will protect her entire family from failures in observance of the commandments. She will then be able, with the extra measure of understanding that has been granted to women, to positively influence her family and make her home a dwelling place for God's presence.

The Rebbe writes:
Likkutei Sichot vol. 3, pp. 749-750

Our Sages say that when God gave the Torah, He told Moses, "So shall you say to the House of Jacob,"[6] and they interpret the phrase "the House of Jacob" to refer to the women. Thus, God was instructing Moses to speak first to the women about receiving the Torah, in order to prevent the failure that occurred in connection with the sin of eating from the Tree of Knowledge. Only Adam — and not Eve — heard the commandment not to eat from that tree directly from God, and this situation allowed the possibility of failure.

Eve was created directly by God Himself, and her body was built using one of the ribs of Adam, who was created directly by the hands of God. Nevertheless, because Eve did not hear the commandment from God Himself, she found it possible to add to the commandment the words "and do not touch it." This addition of hers led to the sin of the Tree of Knowledge. If the commandment had been given directly to her, not only would she not have done the sin, she would also have influenced Adam not to stumble into doing that sin, even though the evil inclination strongly urged them to do it. We see this from the statement of our Sages regarding the giving of the Torah, which was described earlier.

As previously mentioned, the stories in the Torah (the word "Torah" is related to the word *"hora'ah"* — teaching) in *Parashat Bereishit* constitute general instructions for the entire year. The above-mentioned idea is also a lesson regarding how a Jewish home should be conducted.

Every Jewish home must be analogous to a "miniature Sanctuary," about which God can say, "I will dwell among them"[7], i.e., "I will dwell there." Since the conduct of the home depends on the *akeret habayit*, we must exert an

---

6   Exodus 19:3, [translation is from *Artscroll Tanach*, Mesorah Publications, Ltd., Brooklyn, New York, 2003]
7   [Exodus 25:8]

influence specifically on her — not in a manner of "I have made a decree," but rather in pleasant and peaceful ways — to make her have an enthusiasm and a taste for Judaism. Through this, she will prevent the entire household, including her husband, from stumbling into transgressions. As mentioned earlier, if Eve herself had heard the commandment from God, then not only would she have not brought about any stumbling into transgression, but on the contrary, she would have protected Adam from the deceptive words of the snake.

Therefore, the first priority must be, "So shall you say to the House of Jacob" — involving oneself with the members of the household. The statement of the Rebbe Rashab[8] is well known: "Just as putting on *tefillin* every day is a commandment of the Torah which is obligatory for every [male] Jew, regardless of whether he is very learned in Torah or a simple man, it is also an absolute obligation for every Jew to spend a half hour every day thinking about the education and guidance of his children, and to do everything that is within his power, and even more than what is within his power, to influence his children to follow the path on which we are guiding them."

Then, "and relate to the sons of Israel"[6] — the communication of God's commandments to the men — will be fulfilled. That is because then not only will the wife not be "an opponent to him"[9] — she will not disturb her husband — but on the contrary, she will be a "helper."[10] She will assist him by using her special quality of "An additional measure of understanding was given to the woman as compared to the man."[11] She will then also make the entire house a place

---

8   [Rabbi Sholom Dovber, the fifth Lubavitcher Rebbe.]
9   [This phrase is one translation of the word *kenegdo* in the verse that describes God's plan for how the wife will relate to her husband (Genesis 2:18).]
10   [Genesis 2:18]
11   *Nidda* 45b

where God's presence can dwell — "I will dwell among them."

STUDY QUESTIONS:

1. Why did God instruct Moses to speak first to the women about receiving the Torah?

2. Even though Eve was created directly by God, what circumstances made it possible for her to mislead Adam?

3. What approach to the *akeret habayit*'s performance of mitzvot would help her prevent such a mishap?

4. What activity should every parent perform daily to promote their children's education?

5. What special talent can the woman use to enhance the spiritual environment in the home?

Parashat Noach

INFLUENCING THE WORLD
IN A PLEASANT WAY

In *Parashat Noach*, God commanded Noach and his sons to have many children: "God blessed Noach and his sons, and He said to them, 'Be fruitful and multiply, and fill the land...And you, be fruitful and multiply, teem on the earth and multiply on it.' "[12] The question arises: Why does God repeat this commandment here, in *Parashat Noach*, when He already gave this commandment to Adam and Eve earlier, in *Parashat Bereishit*? As it states: "God blessed them, and God said to them, 'Be fruitful and multiply, fill the earth and subdue it...' "[13]

In the discourse from which the following section is excerpted, the Rebbe discusses and answers the above-mentioned question. The Rebbe points out that the command in *Parashat Bereishit* was given before the flood in the time of Noach, whereas the command in *Parashat Noach* was given after. The Rebbe explains that the flood brought about a fundamental change in the world. Before the flood, the only way to bring about any change was by using force, by imposing one's will. Therefore, in the commandment in *Parashat Bereishit*, God uses the words "subdue it." However, the flood had a purifying effect on the world, so that after the flood, a new approach to changing the world became possible. Now, one could do so by refining and purifying. That is why the command in *Parashat Noach* does not include the words "subdue it."

---

12   Genesis 9:1, 7
13   Genesis 1:28

In the section from the discourse presented below, the Rebbe explains that since the time of the flood, both approaches to changing the world are applicable. However, the approach of refining and purifying is the feminine approach. As our Sages have said, "It is the way of a man to conquer, and it is not the way of a woman to conquer."[14]

A woman's main influence is in the home – her focus is her family. From there, her influence projects out into the world and thus gives the woman an important role in shaping it. Furthermore, the type of gentle, pleasant influence she uses is actually more powerful than the aggressive, masculine approach, since the subject accepts this kind of influence willingly. The Rebbe ends this discourse with the wish that in the merit of the good deeds of the women of our generation, performed in the gentle and refined manner characteristic of women, the true and complete redemption should come speedily.

The Rebbe writes:
Sefer HaSichot 5751, pp.84-86

It is easily understandable that a woman and a Jewish daughter were created (just as a man was) to take over and "conquer" her portion of the world. In particular, since she is an *akeret habayit*, (and similarly, also the daughter who is being trained for this role) it is incumbent upon her to "conquer" and be a master over her home and her entire household, and to illuminate them with, "the lamp of the commandment and the light of Torah."[15] Actually, the main part and the beginning of the service of "conquering" starts in the home, and only <u>afterwards</u> does it extend to outside the home (through the husband whose manner it is to conquer). The conquests of a king proceed in the same way — he first conquers his own country, and afterward, other countries (a

---

14   *Yevamot* 65b
15   Proverbs 6:23

foolish king conquers other countries before his own country).

One can conclude that the statement of our Sages that, "It is the way of a man to conquer, and it is not the way of a woman to conquer," refers to the difference in the manner and procedure of a man's conquest and a woman's conquest.

The simple meaning of conquering is compelling the subject against his will by going out to battle with him in a strong and powerful way and at times, with shouting. This is the way of a man: "It is the way of a man to conquer," but it is not the way of a woman: "...and it is not the way of a woman to conquer" (in the way that a man conquers), since "the honor of a king's daughter is internal."[16] Her way [of conquering] is not through <u>going out</u> in a strong and powerful way (which sometimes involves arrogance), being bold, etc.

However, the aspect of conquering in which one conquers and transforms the spiritually lowly world (which on its own is not receptive to Godliness) into a dwelling place for God — this aspect is a characteristic of a woman also.

Moreover, the conquering of a woman is without bringing in influences outside herself and outside her boundaries, but rather in a manner of "the honor of a king's daughter is internal," specifically "internal." That is, internal in location, since her work is mainly inside the home (in her role as *akeret habayit*), as well as internal in substance, since her manner of conduct is not with strength and power, but rather with an inner refinement and honor — in a way of honor, politeness and restfulness.

From this, however, it is understood that a woman does not have any deficiency compared to a man, but on the contrary: her manner of conduct has an advantage over the man's manner of conduct. The fact that "it is the way of a man

---

16   Psalms 45:14

to conquer" shows that the principal way that he exerts an influence is through conquering and dominion and not through "they accepted His kingship <u>willingly</u>"[17]. Because of deficiency in the lowly world, as well as deficiency in his own capability, his influence is a superficial influence the way people's service of God was before the Flood. This is not the case with a woman, because "it is not her way to conquer." She exerts an influence in an internal way, in a way of honor and politeness, in a way of tranquility. She employs an internal influence, such that the one who is being influenced willingly accepts the influence (the advantage of people's service of God after the Flood).

As we see in practical terms, when one speaks with another person with honor and politeness, in a pleasant and peaceful way, one influences him very much more than he would if he shouts at the other person and frightens him and tries to force him "this way and not in any other way." Therefore, this manner of conduct of Jewish women and girls is also a lesson and a guide for men and boys on how they should conduct themselves — specifically in a way of honor, in an internal way.

STUDY QUESTIONS:

1. What role does the woman play in "conquering" her home?

2. What is the difference between a man's way of conquering and a woman's way?

3. What behaviors are typical of the two ways of conquering?

4. Which approach to conquering is most effective?

---

17 [This phrase is from the *Ma'ariv* (evening) prayer.]

5.   How does the subject of the conquering feel about each of the two approaches?

Parashat Lech Lecha

A MAN'S WEALTH IS EARNED
THROUGH THE MERIT OF HIS WIFE

In *Parashat Lech Lecha*, Abram[18] and Sarai[19] arrived in the promised land of Canaan, only to find that there was a famine there. They traveled to Egypt in search of food, and upon their arrival, Abram made a request of Sarai. Because she was so beautiful, he asked her to say that she was his sister, rather than his wife. Then the Egyptians would not kill him in order to take her for themselves and they would give him gifts because of her. He stated his request to her as follows: "Please say that you are my sister, that it may go well with me for your sake, and that I may live on account of you."[20] Sarai agreed to Abram's request and said that she was his sister. Pharaoh's officers then took her away to Pharaoh's palace, apparently in the hope of making her a wife for Pharaoh.

This request that Abram made raises some questions. How could Abram put Sarai into such an unpleasant and dangerous situation in order to save himself? Furthermore, the first reason Abram mentioned in his request is that it would go well with him, that the Egyptians would give him gifts (*Rashi*'s interpretation)! How could he put her in such a situation so that he could receive gifts and mention that as his primary reason?

In the discourse excerpted below, the Rebbe discusses the *Zohar*'s answers to these questions. He explains that on the spiritual level, the purpose of Abram's trip to Egypt was to

---

18   Abram was the original name of the patriarch Abraham before God changed it.
19   Sarai was the original name of the matriarch Sarah before God changed it.
20   Genesis 12:13

refine sparks of holiness that were found there and he accomplished this by receiving gifts from the Egyptians. However, the *Zohar* points out that it is in the merit of a man's wife that he earns money. Therefore, he had to let his wife Sarai be taken to Pharaoh's palace; he couldn't have received the gifts and refined the sparks of holiness through his own merits alone. Also, he was sure that her great merit would protect her from being harmed while in Pharaoh's palace.

This discourse shows the great privilege that the wife has as being the one in whose merit her husband earns money.[21]

The Rebbe writes:
Likkutei Sichot vol. 20, pp. 38-40

Regarding the statement that Abraham made to Sarah before they arrived in Egypt,

> "And it shall occur, when the Egyptians will see you, they will say, "This is his wife"; then they will kill me, but you they will let live. Please say that you are my sister, that it may go well with me for your sake, and that I may live on account of you."[22]

there is a well-known question: How could Abraham place Sarah in a situation in which the Egyptians would take her away, in order that <u>he</u> should be saved by doing so? The commentaries explain that Abraham did not commit any transgression by doing so, and the *Zohar* states that Abraham was certain that Sarah's merit would help her and that she would not be harmed. However, it is completely incomprehensible that Abraham concluded, "...that it may <u>go well with me</u> for your sake." This means that because of her statement that she is his sister, he will be given <u>gifts</u>. How could it be that when contemplating such a serious issue, —

---

21 For insight into the practical aspect of *how* her merit brings material blessings to the family, please refer to the chapter on *Parashat Re'ei.(page 231)*

22 Genesis 12:12-13

placing Sarah in such an undesirable situation in order to save himself from mortal danger — that receiving gifts should be of any significance (to the extent that this was actually the first reason he gave for his request: "Please say that you are my sister, <u>in order that</u> it may go well with me for your sake")?

The *Zohar* addresses this issue, and asks, "Could it be that Abraham, who feared sin and loved God, would say such a thing about his wife in order that <u>they would benefit him</u>?" The *Zohar* answers that Abraham "did not rely on his own merit and he did not make a request from God based on his own merit. Instead, he relied on his wife's merit, that he would acquire <u>in her merit the wealth</u> of the other nations, for a man merits wealth for his wife's sake" (and it explains in detail how through a "wise wife" a man "merits everything"). The *Zohar* then continues, "and he relied on her merit that they would not be able to punish him and to mock her. Because of this, he was not at all afraid to say, 'She is my sister.'"

This too requires explanation. The *Zohar*'s main question, "Could it be that Abraham...would say such a thing about his wife in order that they would benefit him?" means, as mentioned above: How could Abraham have placed his wife (Sarah) in such a situation "in order that <u>they would benefit him</u>"? The simple answer is that Abraham was certain "that they would not be able to... mock her," and therefore, "he was not at all afraid to say, 'She is my sister.'" If so, then why does the *Zohar* say — at the beginning of the answer — that Abraham was certain that "he would acquire in her merit the wealth," and explains this at length, whereas the *Zohar* mentions the main answer — that he was certain that no one would be able to harm her — only at the end? Even more so: In the beginning of the answer, the *Zohar* says, "He did not rely on his own merit and he did not make a request from God based on his own merit. Instead..." This does not seem to have any relevance to the answer of the question, "Could it be that Abraham...would say such a thing about his wife in order that they would benefit him?"

The explanation is as follows. God had said to Abraham that through his obedience of the command, "Go for yourself from your land..."[23] he would merit fulfillment of the promise, "And I will make of you a great nation, I will bless you, and make your name great."[24] According to *Rashi*'s commentary on this verse, "I will bless you" means he will be blessed with wealth. Therefore, Abraham figured that God's setting up events in such a way that he had to leave the Land of Israel (God "induced him to go out from it"[25]) and go down to Egypt is connected with the fulfillment of the promise, "I will bless you," which is brought about through "*Lech Lecha* — Go for yourself." Since he saw a way that the promise, "I will bless you" with wealth could be fulfilled through natural means in Egypt — through Sarah's saying that she is his sister — he therefore said, "Please say that you are my sister, so that it may go well with me for your sake." It actually turned out that way. Once she said that she was his sister, "He [Pharaoh] treated Abram well for her sake, and he acquired sheep, cattle, donkeys..."[26]

Just as the events turned out this way according to the plain meaning of the verses, so too, on a deeper level of meaning, the verses have an analogous explanation. Through "Go for yourself," Abraham had to ascend to higher spiritual levels through refining and elevating the sparks of holiness in the world. Abraham's descent to Egypt also had this purpose, to refine the sparks of holiness that were present there.

---

23   Genesis 12:1

24   Genesis 12:2

25   *Rashi* on Genesis 12:10, [*The Pentateuch and Rashi's Commentary, A Linear Translation into English* by Rabbi Abraham ben Isaiah and Rabbi Benjamin Sharfman; S.S. & R. Publishing Company; Brooklyn, NY, 1977]

26   Genesis 12:16, [*Artscroll Tanach*, Mesorah Publications, Ltd., Brooklyn, New York, 2003]

Since the commandments, whose purpose is the refinement of sparks of holiness in the world, must generally be carried out through natural means, therefore Abraham told Sarah, "Please say that you are my sister." Through that approach, the purpose of his descent to Egypt (the spiritual ascent he would attain through refinement of the sparks) would be accomplished in a natural way, "...in order that it may go well with me for your sake."

The *Zohar's* question is: According to the above-mentioned approach, the result would be "...that it may <u>be well with me</u>," the "it may be well" (the spiritual ascent through refinement of the sparks) would accrue only to Abraham and not to Sarah. Even worse, Sarah would be among the Egyptians ("The woman was taken to Pharaoh's house"[27]), although they would not harm her.

The question is: How can one say that Abraham should cause such a great descent to Sarah (to be in Pharaoh's house) in order that *he* should ascend? Although it was clear to Abraham that the ultimate purpose of his descent to Egypt was for the purpose of the ascent — "...that it may go well with me," nevertheless, God can accomplish something in several different ways. Shouldn't Abraham have trusted in God that this could be accomplished in some other way and not through the descent of Sarah?

The *Zohar* answers this by saying, "He did not rely on his own merit...Instead, he relied on his wife' s merit, that he would acquire <u>in her merit</u> the wealth...for a man merits wealth for <u>his wife's</u> sake" — the man merits earning wealth through "his wife." From this the analogous spiritual explanation is understood. In order for the ascent through refining the sparks in Egypt to be accomplished, <u>his descent</u> to Egypt was not sufficient. He could not rely on his own merit, but rather there must be the merit of his wife. It is specifically through <u>her descent</u> to "Pharaoh's house" that the

---

27   Genesis 12:15

sparks will be elevated ("that he would acquire <u>in her merit</u> the wealth of the other nations").

Since the ultimate purpose for the descent is the ascent that will be accomplished through the "wise wife," Sarah, it is understood that in her merit they will not be able to <u>punish him</u> (it will not lead to any descent for Abraham) or to <u>mock her</u> (or to cause any descent for Sarah).

STUDY QUESTIONS:

1.   As Abraham and Sarah approached Egypt, what request did Abraham make of Sarah, and what two reasons did he give for this request?

2.   What is surprising about Abraham's request of Sarah?

3.   What are the two answers that the Zohar gives to explain why Abraham's request was justified?

4.   According to the Zohar, in whose merit would Abraham acquire wealth in Egypt?

5.   Although the intent of the journey of Abraham and Sarah to Egypt was to obtain food, what was the deeper intent of their journey?

6.   Why did Abraham need Sarah's involvement in order to accomplish the deeper intent?

Parashat Vayeira

BRINGING UP ONE'S CHILDREN
ACCORDING TO THE HIGHEST STANDARD

Parashat Vayeira describes the birth and childhood of our forefather Isaac, son of Abraham and Sarah. As Isaac grew older, Sarah observed the behavior of Ishmael, son of Abraham and Hagar, Abraham's Egyptian maid and concubine. Sarah noticed that Ishmael was growing up to have a bad character and that he was committing serious transgressions. Since he was likely to have a bad influence on her son Isaac, she decided to send Hagar and Ishmael away from her home[28]. Although Abraham found it difficult to agree with her decision, God instructed him to follow Sarah's opinion. We see that Sarah made the greatest effort possible to ensure a proper upbringing for her son, Isaac.

In the excerpt below, the Rebbe describes the great influence a mother has on the upbringing of her children. He tells Jewish mothers that they must bring up their children according to the highest standards possible and that they must not allow themselves to be satisfied with anything less. Mothers must raise their children with such a degree of holiness that they attain the spiritual level of a *Kohen Gadol*. Only when a mother exerts herself to such a degree is she truly fulfilling God's will.

---

28   Rabbi Aharon Kotler, quoted in *The Midrash Says, Bereishit*, p. 186, Rabbi Moshe Weissman, Bnai Yakov Publications, New York, 1980.

The Rebbe writes:
Likkutei Sichot vol. 2, pp. 319-320

"One of the principal aspects in the conduct of Jewish women, which influences their sons and daughters, is the concept of *tzniut* (modesty): "The honor of a king's daughter is internal[29] (in privacy)." As the Gemara tells us regarding the extraordinary *tzniut* of Kimchit (a mother of *Kohanim Gedolim* in the time of the *Beit Hamikdash*), the walls of her house never saw the hairs on her head. Because of this, she merited to have seven of her sons serve as *Kohanim Gedolim* in the *Beit Hamikdash*.

One should not think, 'Why should I conduct myself with such a high level of *tzniut* just so that my children should be *Kohanim Gedolim*? What is wrong with them being ordinary *kohanim*? After all, all Jews are holy!'

The lighting of the Menorah teaches us about this idea. The Menorah must give light specifically in the *heichal*[30]; as mentioned earlier in this discourse, if there is a possibility, it must give light in a place of superior holiness. In our context, if a woman has the opportunity to raise her children to be *Kohanim Gedolim*, that itself is a proof that it is her obligation to do so and if she does not carry out this task, then she would have completely failed to do her duty. She would not have carried out God's will.

This applies especially to Jewish women, because the education of their sons and daughters depends on them. They must realize that their own conduct must be in such a manner and to such an extent that they are able to bring up their children to be *Kohanim Gedolim*.

---

29   Psalms 45:14
30   [The *heichal* was the part of the Holy Temple in which the holiest items, including the Menorah, were kept.]

Our Sages say regarding a *Kohen Gadol* that we must make him great.[31] Through the above-mentioned conduct, all hindrances and obstacles in the lives of the sons and the daughters will be nullified – one will be blessed with an abundance of children, life, and sustenance in the literal sense.

STUDY QUESTIONS:

1.   What mitzvah does the Rebbe mention as an example of a way in which a mother can strongly influence her children?

2.   What woman does the Rebbe mention as an example of someone who excelled in performance of this mitzvah, and what was her reward for her exemplary performance?

3.   What objection might someone raise regarding the applicability of this women's standard of behavior to his or her own behavior?

4.   What proof does the Rebbe give that one must strive to raise one's children according to the highest possible standard of mitzvah observance?

5.   Why does this discussion have a special relevance to Jewish women?

---

31   *Yoma* 18a. That is, he must be made great, endowed, to the point of being the greatest and most elevated among his brethren (fellow *kohanim*), both spiritually and materially. [This footnote was taken from Rabbi Menachem. M. Schneerson, *Likkutei Sichot* (English translation), Volume 4: *Bamidbar*, p. 106, Kehot Publication Society, Brooklyn, New York, 1992.]

6.   What is the reward for making an effort to raise one's children according to the highest possible standard of mitzvah observance?

Parashat Chayei Sarah

SERVING GOD WITH ALL OF ONE'S ABILITIES

The first verse in *Parashat Chayei Sarah* summarizes the lifetime of the Matriarch Sarah, "Sarah's lifetime was one hundred years, twenty years, and seven years; the years of Sarah's life."[32] *Rashi* asks 'Why is the word "years" repeated so many times in this verse?' It seems that the verse could have stated more concisely that the years of Sarah's life were one hundred twenty-seven years. *Rashi* answers that each phrase in the verse tells us about a special quality of Sarah's life. At the age of one hundred, she was as sinless as a twenty year old, for until the age of twenty, a person does not suffer Heavenly punishment. At the age of twenty, she still had the natural beauty of a seven year old. This explanation shows how at each stage in her life she served God at a very high level.

In the excerpt below, the Rebbe teaches us some lessons we can learn from *Rashi's* explanation. The Rebbe describes how at each stage in her life Sarah served God to the best of her ability; she was always achieving her full potential. Furthermore, her service in her later years was so perfect that it retroactively elevated her service from her earlier years to the same high level that had only been achieved later.

The Rebbe points out that these features of Sarah's life have a special relevance to Jewish women. A Jewish woman must make sure that at any given time in her life she is serving God with all of the powers and abilities that she possesses. In the earlier sections of the discourse, the Rebbe presents the following question, 'We know that during Sarah's lifetime, she was continually ascending to higher

---

32   Genesis 23:1

spiritual levels. If so, then how can *Rashi* say that they were all *equally* good?"

The Rebbe writes:
Likkutei Sichot vol. 20, pp. 326-328

From the fact that *Rashi* says, "When she was one hundred years old, she was as free of sin as a twenty year old; when she was twenty years old, she was as beautiful as a seven year old," one can understand that she was on a higher level when she was twenty than she was at age seven, and that she was at a higher level at age one hundred than she was at age twenty."

The explanation of this is that during the years when she was older than seven, her beauty was [miraculously] renewed (because the nature of the body is that as it ages, its beauty diminishes). Therefore, at that time, her service of God must have been on such a high level that it caused a change in the nature of her body.

Similarly, regarding her years after twenty, the fact that she remained without sin was due to her extraordinary service of God. There must have been an increase and a higher level in her service of God during that time, relative to what it was before she was twenty.

Also, regarding her final twenty-seven years, after she had already reached the level of "one hundred years," a number that represents completeness and perfection of service of God, her service of God was then on a level of perfection.

Moreover, at the time of her passing away from this world, she was on an even higher level. That is because in addition to the fact that at the time of one's passing, "all of one's actions that he did all the days of his life" are gathered together, she was then on a very high level, due to "the news of the *Akeidah* (Isaac's being bound on the altar)."

Based on all the above, *Rashi*'s statement, they were "all equal in goodness," is incomprehensible. How can we say that her first seven years (which include even her first year) were <u>equal to</u> her final years (including the years after one hundred years), up to the time of her passing away from this world?

The explanation of all of this is that everything that Sarah did in her service of God was done at the ultimate degree of perfection, in accordance with the strength and capabilities that she had <u>at that time</u>. Therefore, they were all "equally good," for in all of her actions she perfectly fulfilled God's requests, being that "He only requests of the person according to his abilities."[33]

However, this explanation is insufficient, for it implies that all her <u>deeds</u> were <u>equal</u> in goodness. By contrast, the verse praises Sarah by repeating the phrase, "The <u>years</u> of Sarah's life," which "were all equal in goodness." From this it follows that Sarah accomplished something special in connection with the years of her life. The explanation is as follows: Sarah's service of God was always complete to the ultimate extent (in accordance with her capabilities at that particular time). Yet, in addition to this, her service of God achieved perfection in her <u>years</u>. This means that the service of God of her earlier years was for her a preparation for the higher-level service of her later years.

Similarly, the other way around: her service of God of her later years was (not only on a higher level, according to her capabilities that she had at that time, but also) done in such a way that she elevated her prior service and years, so that they were elevated to the higher level (the level at which she was in her later years).

Since her earlier years were eventually uplifted to the very high level that she experienced at the time of her passing away from this world, therefore (after they had been elevated), "they were all equal in goodness."

---

33 *Bamidbar Rabbah* Ch. 12, sec. 3

The statement, "they were all equal in goodness," refers to Sarah, (that through her service, she elevated her prior years and service to the higher level, as mentioned). However, since this is stated in the Torah,[34] it serves as a lesson (and an empowerment) to every Jew (particularly for Jewish women and daughters, each of whom is called "a daughter of Sarah"). The lesson is that as we grow older and increase our understanding and strength in the service of God, we should elevate the years and the Torah and *mitzvot* that we had done previously (before we acquired the increased understanding and strength). One might incorrectly reason that even if a person strives each day (according to his capability on that day) to perfect his service of God, this service of God (and the time in which it was performed) will eventually have to be elevated to the higher level, at which he will arrive later. Therefore, it is not so important to strive each day, with all of one's capability, that his service should be perfect. Even if something is "missing" in one's service of God, one has the ability to perfect it later. The correct understanding is derived from the order of the topics in the verse. First, the verse says, "One hundred years, twenty years and seven years." *Rashi* explains, "The word 'years' is written in connection with each enumeration in order to tell you that each enumeration has its own explanation." That is, every individual time must be perfected in itself, in accordance with the level of strength one is given at that time. Only then, does the verse state, "The years of Sarah's life," which means according to *Rashi*, "They were all equal in goodness." It is specifically through the perfection of each <u>individual</u> time that one can afterwards be elevated to the higher level of the later time.

---

34 [As mentioned previously, the word 'Torah' is grammatically related to the word *hora'ah*, which means 'instruction.']

STUDY QUESTIONS:

1. What seems peculiar about the verse that tells how old Sarah was when she passed away?

2. What were Sarah's major accomplishments at the various stages of her life, according to Rashi's explanation of the verse?

3. What does the Rebbe say about Sarah's spiritual level as she progressed through her life?

4. In view of the answer to question #3, how does the Rebbe explain Rashi's statement that all of Sarah's years were equally good?

5. What lesson can we derive from the example of Sarah's life for the conduct of our own lives?

6. What erroneous conclusion might one draw from our examination of Sarah's life, and how could we avoid drawing this conclusion?

Parashat Toldot

A WIFE'S INFLUENCE ON HER HUSBAND

In *Parashat Toldot*, we see two examples of how Rebecca had both a strong and a positive influence on her husband, Isaac. The first example of positive influence was when Isaac asked Esau to prepare food for him so that he could bless Esau afterward. When Rebecca heard this request, she gave Jacob instructions to follow so that *he* should get the blessing instead of Esau. Although Isaac initially blessed Jacob unknowingly, Isaac confirmed the blessing when he learned what had happened.[35] Thus, he ultimately arrived at the same conclusion as Rebecca, i.e., that Jacob should be blessed.

The second example of positive influence was when Rebecca realized that Esau wanted to kill Jacob. She decided to send Jacob far away from home until Esau's anger subsided. However, she did not want to tell Isaac about Esau's hatred for Jacob, so she gave him a different reason for wanting to send Jacob away.[36] Thus, she was able to convince Isaac to reach the same conclusion that she did, while not causing him too much grief.

Below, the Rebbe describes how the Jewish wife is the *akeret habayit* – the foundation of the home – and is thus responsible for the conduct of all that takes place within it. Part of this role includes exerting a positive influence on her husband. If she chooses the proper approach — a pleasant and peaceful one — she will accomplish this effectively.

---

35   Genesis 27:33, *Rashi*
36   Genesis 27:46

The Rebbe writes:
Likkutei Sichot vol. 2, pp. 575-576

At the time of the giving of the Torah, the women — referred to as *Beit Yaakov* — were to be the first to receive the new teachings, and the men — referred to as *Bnai Yisrael* — were to receive them only afterwards. The reason the women were to be taught first is that the woman is the *akeret habayit*, the foundation of the Jewish home. Therefore, it is the woman's role to have a positive influence on the man.

A Jewish daughter and woman must know that the conduct of the home depends on her and she must see to it that she has a positive influence on her husband. It is true that a woman is obligated to honor her husband. Nevertheless, if she is determined enough, she will be able to accomplish everything she needs to in a pleasant and peaceful manner.

STUDY QUESTIONS:

1. What are two things that Rebecca did in a peaceful way to help her husband reach the right conclusions?

2. What special role do women have that made them merit to receive the Torah before the men?

3. What responsibility does the woman have toward her husband as a result of her special role in the home?

4. What important factor(s) should a woman keep in mind if she tries to influence her husband?

5. What approach should the woman take if and when she tries to influence her husband?

Parashat Vayeitzei

THE FAR-REACHING EFFECTS OF
HOW A MOTHER RAISES HER CHILDREN

Parashat Vayeitzei describes Jacob's experiences at his uncle Laban's house. Jacob had a difficult time there, because Laban repeatedly deceived and mistreated him. Yet in spite of his troubles, Jacob and his wives raised twelve sons who were all righteous and went on to become the twelve tribes of the Jewish nation.

The Rebbe explains below that it was because of Jacob's wives that he was able to bring up his sons to be righteous. These wives did their utmost to make sure that their homes ran according to the proper values and their efforts affected not only their own children, but also the entire Jewish nation. Thus, the conduct of Jacob's wives provides an example and a lesson for all Jewish mothers. Like Jacob's wives, every Jewish woman has a responsibility toward her own family, as well as to the entire Jewish nation.

The Rebbe writes:
Likkutei Sichot vol. 10, p. 213

The Torah portion of *Vayeitzei* teaches us a great deal regarding the responsibility of the Jewish woman as the *akeret habayit*, not only of her own home, but also of the <u>entire Jewish nation</u>. The Torah portion teaches us that Jacob, our patriarch, arrived in a foreign land and endured difficult times. In spite of all this, he established the foundation for the Jewish nation, such that <u>all</u> of his children remained faithful to the tradition of their fathers, Abraham, Isaac, and Jacob. This was made possible thanks to the fact that the Jewish Mothers — Rachel, Leah, Bilhah, and Zilpah — did everything that depended on them to do in order to ensure the wholesomeness of their home, and the future of their nation.

STUDY QUESTIONS:

1.   In her role as *akeret habayit*, how far does the Jewish woman's responsibility extend?

2.   What are some of the difficulties Jacob faced while raising his children?

3.   What helped Jacob be successful in raising his children properly?

4.   What fact shows that Jacob and his wives did raise their children properly?

5.   What lesson can Jewish women of today draw from the way Rachel, Leah, Bilhah, and Zilpah raised their children?

Parashat Vayishlach

EXERTING A POSITIVE INFLUENCE
ON OTHER JEWISH WOMEN

Parashat Vayishlach describes the story of Dinah, daughter of Jacob and Leah, in Shechem. After Jacob and his family left Laban's house in Charan to go back to Jacob's original home in Hebron, they stopped to set up camp in the city of Shechem. Dinah ventured out to see the girls of Shechem, as the verse states,[37] "Now Dinah — the daughter of Leah, whom she had borne to Jacob — went out to look over the daughters of the land." During her outing, Shechem, a prince in the region, saw her, took a liking to her, and kidnapped her.

Shechem desired to marry Dinah and to establish an arrangement whereby the residents of Shechem could intermarry with members of Jacob's family. Jacob's sons replied that they could not consent to this arrangement unless all males of the city were circumcised, and the condition was agreed upon. While the men of Shechem were in pain from the procedure, Jacob's sons, Simeon and Levi, killed them, captured their women and children and redeemed Dinah.

The discourse, from which the following excerpt is taken, examines Dinah's motivation for her excursion in Shechem in light of *Rashi*'s commentary on Genesis 34:1. *Rashi* compares Dinah's outgoingness to her mother Leah's outgoingness. It might seem that this quality is undesirable, but the Rebbe points out that Leah was outgoing for a good reason. Similarly, Dinah must have had a good reason for her excursion.

---

37   Genesis 34:1

In fact, Dinah had an exceptional talent for positively influencing people. The magnitude of this gift can be seen from the fact that Jacob was punished for withholding Dinah from marrying Esau. Her influence was so powerful that she could have helped Esau repent; preventing this was a grave thing indeed. Since Dinah had such a talent, the Rebbe concludes that Dinah went out to the girls of Shechem to influence them for the better.

From the story of Dinah, one can learn that Jewish women should use their abilities to positively influence other Jewish women who may be misguided. Women should just make sure that when they do go out for this purpose, it is done in a modest manner. The gentle and peaceful approach that women use will give them exceptional success in their efforts.

The Rebbe writes:
Likkutei Sichot vol. 35, pp. 150-151, 154-155

"Now Dinah — the daughter of Leah, whom she had borne to Jacob — went out to look over the daughters of the land."[38] *Rashi* comments on the words "the daughter of Leah," "And was she not the daughter of Jacob? However, because of her 'going forth' she was called 'the daughter of Leah,' for she too was one who goes out (*Bereishit Rabba*) as it is stated, 'And Leah went forth to greet him.'" (According to some texts, *Rashi* adds at the end of his explanation — "And regarding her, they introduced the proverb, 'Like mother, like daughter' [Ezekiel 16:44].")[39]

This explanation seems to require examination. Why did *Rashi*, whose commentary explains the simple meaning of the text, choose this explanation, according to which the text speaks disparagingly of Leah? The Torah does not even speak

---

38   Ibid.
39   [Translation of *Rashi* is from *The Pentateuch and Rashi's Commentary, A Linear Translation into English* by Rabbi Abraham ben Isaiah and Rabbi Benjamin Sharfman; S.S. & R. Publishing Company; Brooklyn, NY, 1977]

disparagingly about an impure animal and *Rashi* has already explained,[40] "The memory of the righteous shall be for a blessing."

It cannot be said that *Rashi's* intention was to argue Dinah's merit by minimizing the disparagement of Dinah, saying that her going out was not her fault, but rather it was due to her being "the daughter of Leah," who was also one who went out. It would not be proper to speak meritoriously about the daughter through mentioning something negative about Leah.

It is possible to explain the repetition in the verse that states, "Now Dinah — the daughter of Leah, whom she had borne to Jacob — went out..." rather than the more concise "the daughter of Jacob." To do this, read in the light of *Rashi's* explanation of a previous verse,[41] where he said that the birth of Dinah came about through the prayer of Leah [while she was pregnant with her fifth child, who was a male at the time when she prayed], who "passed judgment[42] on herself. *Rashi* explains that Leah thought to herself: "If this one will be a male, then my sister Rachel will not even be like one of the maid-servants.", so she prayed regarding him, and he was transformed into a female.

Furthermore, an extreme difficulty with *Rashi's* explanation is: There was nothing undesirable about Leah's going out to greet Jacob. On the contrary, *Rashi* comments on the words, God hearkened to Leah[43] "...For she desired and

---

40 [On Genesis 6:9, *Rashi* comments, "Since it (the Torah) mentions him, it relates his praise, as it is said, 'The memory of the righteous shall be for a blessing' (Proverbs 10:7)." Translation of *Rashi* is from *The Pentateuch and Rashi's Commentary, A Linear Translation into English* by Rabbi Abraham ben Isaiah and Rabbi Benjamin Sharfman; S.S. & R. Publishing Company; Brooklyn, NY, 1977]

41 [Genesis 30:21]

42 [The Hebrew translation for "she passed judgment" is *danna,* which is grammatically related to the name Dinah.]

43 Genesis 30:17

sought to increase tribes."[44] It cannot be said that this going out is something negative and in that sense she is called "one who goes out."

Therefore, it seems that what *Rashi* meant by his commentary on the words, "the daughter of Leah," was that the Torah is telling us that just as by the plain meaning of the text, that Leah's going out was a good thing, similarly, Dinah's going out was in essence something desirable. Thus, *Rashi* does not cite the words of the *Midrash* on this verse, which <u>explicitly describe</u> Dinah's and Leah's lack of modesty. Neither does *Rashi* need to specify what is good about Dinah's going out, because it is understandable according to *Rashi*'s earlier explanation that there is a good reason for it.

The explanation of this is as follows.

Earlier in this Torah portion, *Rashi* explained the meaning of a different verse related to this topic. On the verse, "And he [Jacob] took...and his eleven sons,"[45] *Rashi* explains, "But where was Dinah? He placed her in a chest and locked her in, lest Esau cast his eyes upon her, and for this Jacob was punished, for he withheld her from his brother — for perhaps she would have led him back to the right way — and she fell into the hands of Shechem."[46]

This is very surprising. Could it be that God expected Jacob to endanger Dinah based only on the speculation that "perhaps she would have led him back to the right way?" Furthermore, how could it be that because he did not let Esau see her, Jacob was punished with such a severe punishment that "she fell into the hands of Shechem?"

---

44 [Translation of *Rashi* is from *The Pentateuch and Rashi's Commentary, A Linear Translation into English* by Rabbi Abraham ben Isaiah and Rabbi Benjamin Sharfman; S.S. & R. Publishing Company; Brooklyn, NY, 1977]

45 Genesis 32:23

46 [Translation of *Rashi* is from *The Pentateuch and Rashi's Commentary, A Linear Translation into English* by Rabbi Abraham ben Isaiah and Rabbi Benjamin Sharfman; S.S. & R. Publishing Company; Brooklyn, NY, 1977]

Thus, it seems that: (a) Dinah's special qualities were so great that she had the power to lead the wicked Esau back to the right way and (b) leading a wicked person back on the right path is such an important thing, that it would have been worth involving Dinah, even if the outcome was not assured — "<u>perhaps</u> she would have led him back to the right way."

Furthermore, the fact that Jacob was punished for this, as described above, seems to imply that there was actually no doubt, but rather it was clear that she would have led him back on the right path. *Rashi*'s writing, "<u>perhaps</u> she would have led him back to the right way," was from Jacob's point of view — Jacob could not establish with <u>certainty</u> that she would have led him back to the proper path, because the matter ultimately depended upon Esau's free choice.

According to this explanation of *Rashi*, it is possible to say that *Rashi*'s explanation of the verse discussed here [Genesis 34:1] regarding Dinah's going out is actually a <u>favorable</u> description of Dinah. Since Dinah had the power to lead even the wicked Esau back to the right way, it follows that Dinah's going out "to look over the daughters of the land" was not an immodest going-out. On the contrary, she went out "to look over the daughters of the land" in order to lead them back onto the right path.

That which *Rashi* wrote, "because of her 'going forth' she was called 'the daughter of Leah,' for she too was one who goes out," means that this positive characteristic of Dinah — that she was able to go out to look over the daughters of the land and to lead them back to the right way — comes to her from her mother, who also went out in this manner.

The reason that *Rashi* emphasizes, "...*the daughter of Leah*: And was she not the daughter of Jacob?" [*Rashi* on Genesis 34:1], is because Dinah inherited and received this quality from Leah. In contrast, Jacob behaved in the opposite manner. He hid her from Esau, and prevented her from acting according to this quality, so that Jacob was punished for this, as described earlier.

* * *

It is possible to add that even though in actuality Dinah encountered a pitfall, the reason for it was, as *Rashi* explains (as mentioned earlier),[47] that it was a punishment for Jacob's holding her back from his brother. From this fact itself, it is understood that her going out was not an undesirable act, because the intention behind it was for the sake of Heaven, to lead "the daughters of the land" back to the right way.

Perhaps it can be said that this matter — that her going out was in order to lead them back on the right path, and that it was a good thing — was manifested in the fact that an outcome that reflected Dinah's true goal <u>actually took place</u>. The sons of Jacob influenced the men of Shechem to circumcise all of the males, which is part of the process of conversion that was used in those days to join the family of Abraham. It can be simply understood that this joining was not just for the men, but it was also for the "daughters of the land," the women and the girls, as the verse states explicitly, "On this condition will we acquiesce to you...to become circumcised...<u>and take your daughters to ourselves</u>..."[48]

That is to say: in actuality, the people of Shechem incurred the death penalty because of their sin and therefore they were killed by Simeon and Levi, Dinah's brothers. Nevertheless, in order that the will of that righteous woman, "Dinah, the daughter of Leah," would be fulfilled at least in a small measure, they were circumcised before they were killed. This was a sign of establishment of a covenant with the family of Abraham.

Furthermore, the daughters of Shechem — to whom Dinah went out in order to lead them back to the right way —

47   [On Genesis 32:23]
48   Genesis 34:15-16, [*Artscroll Tanach,* Mesorah Publications, Ltd., Brooklyn, New York, 2003]

were taken prisoner by the sons of Jacob and it can be assumed that they became maidservants in the homes of Jacob's sons.

From this, a lesson for Jewish women can be derived: "The honor of a king's daughter is internal (within)"[49] and the woman is called *akeret habayit*, because her main duty is to build a Jewish home and for this purpose, she must remain "within" the home. Nevertheless, those women who are gifted with special qualities that allow them to exert influence outside the home as well must utilize those qualities in a modest way for the sake of Heaven, to bring people's hearts close to the service of God and to lead Jewish daughters who are "on the outside" back onto the right path.

It is understood and plainly clear that this effort must be done in a manner that is appropriate for a Jewish daughter and in a modest way, to the extent that, "The honor of a king's daughter is internal," must be recognizable in her "going out." Nevertheless, they must lead the errant Jewish daughters back on the right path, while adhering to the boundaries of modesty to the ultimate extent.

Actually, women's natural closeness and gentleness bring people's hearts close to the service of God more successfully than men. It is apparent in a tangible way that when one convinces another person to come close to God's Torah and to His service in a pleasant and peaceful way, the success is much greater and the effect is absorbed more internally and enduringly than what would be achieved through arguments and fighting, as is the nature of men for "It is the way of a man to conquer."[50]

Since God created women with this character trait, it is understood that they must utilize it fully, not only in the conduct of the home, but also in exerting influence outside

---

49   Psalms 45:14
50   *Rashi*, Genesis 1:28

the home, bringing Jewish daughters close to their Father in Heaven.

STUDY QUESTIONS:

1. What character trait did Dinah share with her mother, Leah?

2. How do we know that Dinah had tremendous powers of influencing other people?

3. What was Dinah's goal in going to meet the girls of Shechem?

4. What type of women should make an effort to exert their influence beyond their homes?

5. What precaution should they take when they do attempt to exert influence beyond their homes?

6. What feature of women's approach makes them quite successful in influencing others?

Parashat Vayeishev

SERVING GOD WITH SELF-SACRIFICE

Parashat Vayeishev relates the story of Judah and Tamar. Tamar married Judah's oldest son, Er. Er died without children, so Judah had his next son, Onan, marry Tamar. Onan also died childless. Judah had a third son, but did not let him marry Tamar out of concern that if he married her, he, too, would die.

Tamar wanted to give birth to a descendant of Judah,[51] foreseeing prophetically that great people would descend from that union. She was disappointed when she realized that she would not be able to marry any of Judah's sons. Therefore, after Judah's wife died, Tamar disguised herself and used devious means in order to have children from Judah himself. When Judah found out that Tamar was pregnant, he did not realize that he was the father of her twin babies. He thought that she must have acted immorally and brought her to court. The judges decided that she had to be burned[52].

Tamar did not want to embarrass Judah by revealing that it was from him that she had become pregnant. She sent a messenger to bring the judges some of Judah's belongings that she had with her. She instructed the messenger to tell them, "By the man to whom these belong, I am with child. Identify, if you please, to whom these belong."[53] *Rashi* explains that she also said to herself, "If he will confess by himself, let him confess, and if not, let them burn me, but let

---

51 *Zohar*, quoted in *The Midrash Says, Bereishit*, p. 364, Rabbi Moshe Weissman, Bnai Yakov Publications, New York, 1980.

52 *The Midrash Says, Bereishit*, p. 366, Rabbi Moshe Weissman, Bnai Yakov Publications, New York, 1980.

53 Genesis 38:25, *Artscroll Tanach*, Mesorah Publications, Ltd., Brooklyn, New York, 2003

me not put him to shame."[54] Judah acknowledged that he was that man and her life was spared.

Tamar was so righteous that she preferred to be killed rather than to embarrass Judah publicly. From this story we learn that it is preferable to be thrown into a fiery furnace than cause someone public embarrassment.

In the excerpt below, the Rebbe explains that there are two ways to serve God. The masculine way is to serve God with one's mind and intellect. The feminine way is to serve God with one's heart and feelings. Under ordinary circumstances, the intellect should govern the feelings and thus the masculine aspect must predominate.

However, when there are obstacles and hindrances to serving God, as there are in the time of the *galut* (exile), then this manner of serving God is not sufficient. Rather, one must serve God with self-sacrifice in order to be able to find the inner strength needed to overcome the obstacles. This type of service draws upon powers that are revealed mainly in the heart rather than in the mind. Thus, when there are obstacles to serving God, the feminine aspect must predominate.

Tamar's willingness to give up her life so as not to embarrass Judah is a prime example of serving God in a manner of self-sacrifice. Women of today have a special capability of following Tamar's example by drawing on their talent of serving God from the heart, in a way that is beyond reason and intellect.

The Rebbe writes:
Likkutei Sichot vol. 30, pp. 145-146

Male and female — man and woman — also correspond to two ways of serving God: service of the mind, and service

---

54   *Rashi*, Genesis 38:25, *The Pentateuch and Rashi's Commentary, A Linear Translation into English* by Rabbi Abraham ben Isaiah and Rabbi Benjamin Sharfman; S.S. & R. Publishing Company; Brooklyn, NY, 1977

of the heart. The difference between a man's and woman's way of serving God is along these lines: the intellectual service is mainly done by the man, whereas the unique quality of the woman is in the area of emotions and character.

Each one of these approaches has an advantage. The advantage of the mind and the intellect is that when a person utilizes them, he sees and grasps with his mind's eye the true nature of the subject as it is, without the admixture of "bribes" and the tendencies of a person's nature. In contrast, the emotions and character traits of a person "grasp" the subject in accordance with the tendencies and desires of the person.

On the other hand, there is an advantage of the emotions and character over the intellect. By nature, the intellect is cold, without excitement, and its scope is therefore measured and limited. In contrast, when a person has strong feelings about some matter, then his warm feeling and excitement about it causes his connection with, and involvement in, the matter to be very strong.

Along these lines is the difference between two ways of establishing precedence, the males before the females, or the females before the males.

In general, the world was created in such a way that "He will rule over you"[55] (males before females), because the desired arrangement is that the mind should rule over the heart.[56] In other words, the character traits must be governed by the mind. Thus, if a person follows the inclinations of his heart, he is liable to impair not only the mind, which is in the head, but also the emotions, which are in the heart itself. Only when the character traits are governed and guided by the mind, which is in the head, are the desires of the heart, and therefore the conduct of the person, as they should be.

---

55 [Genesis 3:16]
56 *Likkutei Amarim — Tanya*, [Rabbi Schneur Zalman of Liadi, Kehot Publication Society, Brooklyn, New York, Chapter 12.]

However, there is a situation in which a person must serve his Creator on a level beyond that which would be indicated by the dictates of reason. Such a situation arises when there are many obscurations, obstacles, and hindrances to serving God. In such a case, it is not sufficient to serve God in a measured and limited way, according to the dictates of reason. Rather, a higher level of service is required, one that is beyond the limitations of the intellect. This type of service is revealed specifically in the service of the <u>heart</u>. And it is known[57] that the essence of the soul is revealed specifically in the heart and not in the mind.

Rashi, in his explanation that Jacob "put the males before the females and Esau put the females before the males,"[58] hinted at the above-mentioned ideas. The service of Jacob, "a simple man who dwells in tents,"[59] is an orderly service, with males before females. In this type of service, the service of the mind comes first, the service of the heart follows, and the heart influences all the other parts of the body.

However, in the service of Esau, "a man of the field,"[60] a place of obscuration of and hindrances to the service of God, the order is reversed, with females before males. That is because in these circumstances, a service that is measured and limited according to the orderly way of conduct is inadequate. Instead, what is needed is a service that is beyond the orderly way and beyond measures and limitations, as mentioned above.

It is possible that this idea explains the fact that in the time of the future redemption, "The woman will court the

---

57 *Sefer haMa'amorim Taf-Reish-Samach-Vov*, page 60, and further. [Rabbi Shalom Dovber Schneerson, Kehot Publication Society, Brooklyn, New York, 1976.]

58 [*Rashi*, Genesis 31:17. When Jacob helped his family members mount the camels in preparation for traveling, he helped the males (his sons) before the females (his wives) (Genesis 31:17). On the other hand, when Esau traveled, he took the females (his wives) before the males (his sons) (Genesis 36:6).]

59 Genesis 25:27. See *Rashi's* explanation of the word *tam* (simple) in this verse.

60 [Genesis 25:27]

man."[61] All of the revelations of the future redemption depend on our deeds and our service of God during the entire era of the exile. In particular, all of the accomplishments that were achieved through our service during the time of exile will be revealed. One of the main accomplishments of the service in the era of the exile — particularly this final exile (the exile of Esau, the ancestor of the nation of Edom), in which there are many obscurations of and obstacles to the service of God — is the service that involves self-sacrifice. This type of service is beyond reason and understanding and is revealed mainly in the heart.

STUDY QUESTIONS:

1.   What are the two main ways of serving God that are mentioned in this chapter?

2.   What are the advantages of each approach?

3.   Under normal circumstances, which approach should predominate?

4.   Under which type of circumstances should the other approach predominate?

5.   Which type of service did Tamar use when deciding not to reveal that Judah was the father of her babies?

6.   During the time of exile, which type of service must often predominate?

---

61   [Jeremiah 31:21. This concept indicates a superiority of the feminine aspect at the time of the future redemption.]

7.   How does this type of service overcome the obstacles
      to serving God?

Parashat Mikeitz

ILLUMINATING THE HOME WITH TORAH
EVEN WHEN THERE ARE DIFFICULTIES

Parashat Mikeitz describes Joseph's rise from prisoner to Pharaoh's chief assistant. During the seven years of plenty, Joseph, in his new position, gathered and stored food for Pharaoh in preparation for the impending famine. Joseph also married Asenath, who bore him two sons, Menashe and Ephraim. Sometime later, when the famine began, Joseph was in charge of food distribution, selling food to all of the Egyptians.

Although very little is explicitly mentioned about Asenath in this story, we can surmise that she had a crucial role in the upbringing of her two sons. Joseph was surely very busy with his job as sole distributor of food in the entire land of Egypt. Therefore, Asenath would have had to assume a major role in raising and educating their sons.[62] Moreover, the years of famine were a traumatic time for the Egyptians, since they had to sell all of their belongings, and even themselves, in order to obtain food. During this difficult period, Asenath must have faced spiritual challenges in bringing up her children. However, she did overcome these challenges, and managed to raise her sons to be great men, eventually counted as two of the twelve tribes of the Jewish nation.

The Rebbe explains below that it is up to the *akeret habayit* to ensure that her home is illuminated with the light of Torah and *mitzvot*, even in situations where, God forbid, the family

---

62   In fact, it was Asenath who advised Joseph to bring their children to receive Jacob's blessing shortly before Jacob passed away. (*Midrash*, quoted in *The Midrash Says*, vol. *Bereishit*, p. 441, Rabbi Moshe Weissman, Bnai Yakov Publications, New York, 1980.)

faces the challenge of lacking some material necessity. The husband and children will as a result derive the strength needed to face the pressures outside the home, however difficult they may be. Asenath was a prime example of an *akeret habayit* who illuminated her home with Torah values even during a time of hardship.

The Rebbe writes:
Likkutei Sichot vol. 17, p. 523

The atmosphere of the Jewish home is largely the domain of the wife and mother, the *akeret habayit*. If it seems that some material necessities are lacking, or if it is actually so, God forbid, then it is up to the *akeret habayit* to ensure that this situation does not affect the atmosphere in the home. She must ensure that the home atmosphere is always permeated with the light of Torah and *mitzvot*, with trust in God and with joy, because the atmosphere in the home affects every person in the home. It is from the home that the husband and the children, may they be healthy, draw encouragement and strength to deal with pressures outside the home — the husband, in business matters, and the children, in school.

Since this great privilege and responsibility has been given to the *akeret habayit*, it is certain that she has been given the ability that is necessary to carry it out fully. Such abilities have also been given to Jewish daughters, who are preparing themselves to take their place as *akeret habayit*.

STUDY QUESTIONS:

1. Which family member(s) have the major role in determining the atmosphere in the Jewish home?

2. What can the *akeret habayit* do to ensure that there is a positive atmosphere in the home even if some material necessities may be lacking?

3.   Which member(s) of the family are affected by the atmosphere in the home?

4.   From where do the husband and children draw strength to deal with challenges outside the home?

5.   What makes us sure that the *akeret habayit* does have the strength to create a positive atmosphere in the home?

Parashat Vayigash

TRANSFORMING THE PHYSICAL WORLD
TO MAKE IT DISPLAY GOD'S PRESENCE

Parashat Vayigash describes the descent of the Jewish nation into Egypt. The Torah portion lists the names of the people who went down to Egypt, stating that the total number is seventy. However, if one actually counts the names, there are only sixty-nine. Various commentators offer opinions as to who the seventieth person is.

In the excerpt below, though the Rebbe mentions some of these opinions, he focuses mainly on *Rashi*, who states that the seventieth person was Yocheved – the daughter of Levi and mother of Moses – who was born as the Jews were arriving in Egypt (*Rashi* on Genesis 46:26).

The identity of the seventieth person is not simply another name on the list. It represents the completion of the total. It also represents the culmination of the purpose for which the Jews had to come to Egypt, namely, to make the Egyptians — as well as all of the other nations of the world— recognize that God alone governs the universe.

The Rebbe explains the special significance of the fact that the seventieth person was a female. The feminine way to influence another person is to gently improve and refine the other until he or she comprehends the concept at hand. Contrast this to the masculine approach, which is to compel the other person to accept the concept. In the feminine manner, the person actually becomes transformed into a new person with new attitudes. The fact that the seventieth person was Yocheved, a female, facilitated the transformation of the Egyptians into a nation that recognized God.

The Rebbe concludes the discourse by deriving a lesson applicable to the women of today. In the era of the future redemption, the entire physical world will openly show that its source of existence is Godly. The *mitzvot* that are done by women now have a special ability to transform the physical world into a place that openly displays Godliness, and thus to bring the actual redemption.

The Rebbe writes:
Likkutei Sichot vol. 20, pp. 224-225, 227
(Sections 9, 10, 11, and 13)

The purpose of the descent of the seventy people to Egypt was to bring about a nullification and refinement in the physical world, in the seventy nations of the world and in their seventy heavenly ministers. This nullification and refinement can be accomplished through two different approaches, the masculine and the feminine."

The masculine approach is exemplified by the Talmudic statement, "The way of a man is to conquer."[63] Conquering, in general, involves acting against the will of the one who is being conquered. When something is nullified by being conquered, it is transferred into the control of a different authority, but the thing itself is unchanged.

However, when something is nullified by being purified, the thing itself becomes transformed. This approach characterizes the type of work done by a woman. For example, when she prepares food, she transforms and improves the food so that it becomes fit to eat.

On the spiritual level, either of these two ways could be used to nullify idolatry, specifically, the seventy heavenly ministers, who project their influence into the world. The exile in Egypt brought about and revealed – not only to the Jews, but also to the nations of the world – the fact that the

---

63   *Yevamot* 65b

seventy ministers have no power or authority of their own and further, that they do not even have an independent existence.

In particular, the miracles and the downfall of Pharaoh and Egypt caused even Pharaoh and Egypt to believe and recognize that "I am <u>God</u> in the midst of the <u>land</u>,"[64] and that the stars and planets[65] have no power of their own; they are merely like the ax in the hand of the woodchopper.[66] Even the Egyptian magicians acknowledged,[67] "It is the finger of God."[68]

This nullification of idolatry is accomplished mainly through the attribute of *Malchut* [royalty — the feminine aspect], which is the origin of space and time[69] and the channel through which God influences the seventy ministers. Therefore, these ministers (and thus the seventy nations that correspond to them) perceived that God's kingship has dominion over all, that they have no autonomous existence, and that their existence and rulership is derived solely from the attribute of *Malchut*.

In contrast, from the perspective of the level of Godliness that is higher than this world, the nullification is actualized in such a way that there is no possibility of any existence besides God's, may He be blessed. From the perspective of <u>this</u> level of Godliness, the very existence of the seventy ministers is nullified, to the extent that they are even less substantive than the ax in the hand of the woodchopper.

---

64 Exodus 8:18
65 [The main objects of idol worship in Egypt at that time.]
66 [Although the chopping is accomplished by the motion of the ax, the ax has no power of its own — it is merely an instrument through which the woodchopper exerts his chopping power.]
67 [Referring to one of the ten plagues.]
68 Exodus 8:15
69 *Shaar haYichud vehaEmunah*, [— Tanya, Rabbi Schneur Zalman of Liadi, Kehot Publication Society, Brooklyn, New York,] Chapter 7

This latter perspective represents the idea of conquering, since the nullification of the idolatry does not relate to its particular nature, but rather, it originates from Godliness, which is incomparably higher than the world.

The difference between the two approaches described above corresponds to the difference of opinion between the explanation of *Pirkei deRabbi Eliezer*, "The number of males totaled sixty-six and Joseph with his two sons...God joined in their total," (and along these lines, the opinion that Jacob completed the total), and the opinion that Yocheved completed the total.

The point of view that, "The number of males totaled sixty-six, and Joseph with his two sons..." (i.e., that God or Jacob completed the total) corresponds to the approach of conquering and completely nullifying the existence of idolatry. This type of nullification originates in a level of Godliness that is incomparably higher than this world.

From the perspective of *Malchut*, the feminine quality, the nullification of the idolatry relates to its particular characteristics. Therefore, this approach is more effective than the approach of complete nullification in influencing the gentile nations – in this case Pharaoh and Egypt — to have faith in God. This perspective corresponds to the opinion that the completion of the total of seventy people was accomplished by Yocheved.

At the beginning of the exile in Egypt, it was Yocheved who completed the total of seventy people.[70] Through her, a nullification in the world was accomplished that related to the particular characteristics of the world, as described above.

A similar refinement of the world must take place during this final exile, as a prelude and preparation for the future redemption. At that time, "All flesh shall see...that the mouth

---

70 [According to *Rashi*, whose stated intention was to convey the simple meaning of the text.]

of God has spoken,"[71] the physicality of the world itself will be refined and will "see" the "mouth of God."

A prophecy states[72] regarding the future redemption that God will show us miracles of the type that occurred in the time of the exodus from Egypt. The Jews were redeemed from Egypt in the merit of the righteous women of that generation.[73] Similarly, the future and imminent redemption will be brought about through the service of Jewish women and girls.

We see, therefore, that the three *mitzvot* which were given to Jewish women and girls — lighting Shabbat and *Yom Tov* candles, challah (which also represents *kashrut* of food and drink) and family purity — are of the type that brings about a refinement in the physical world. These *mitzvot* concern activities connected with the type of human needs that must be satisfied in order for the world to be habitable, even by non-Jews: light (so that one does not stumble on obstacles of wood or stone), food and family life.

The job of Jewish women and girls is to make sure that these activities are carried out specifically in a Jewish manner, lighting candles, which is connected with Shabbat and *Yom Tov*, *kashrut* of food and drink, and family purity. Observance of these *mitzvot* is what prepares the physicality of the world to be refined to the extent that all flesh together shall see that the mouth of God has spoken.

STUDY QUESTIONS:

1. What was the purpose of the descent of the Jewish people into Egypt?

---

71 Isaiah 40:5, *Artscroll Tanach*, Mesorah Publications, Ltd., Brooklyn, New York, 2003
72 Micha 7:15
73 *Sotah* 11b; *Bamidbar Rabbah* 3:6

2.   What are the two main approaches to accomplishing this goal?

3.   Which approach corresponds to the opinion that Yocheved was the seventieth member of the group of Jews that entered Egypt?

4.   Which approach is more effective in changing the nature of the one that is to be changed?

5.   What common features do the redemption from Egypt and the future, final redemption share?

6.   How do the three mitzvot that are especially associated with women accomplish the objective that will lead to the future, final redemption?

Parashat Vayechi

GIVING UP ONE'S OWN SPIRITUAL BENEFIT
FOR THE SAKE OF ONE'S CHILDREN

In *Parashat Vayechi*, Jacob asked Joseph not to bury him in Egypt, where he was living at the time. Instead, he asked to be buried in the Cave of Machpelah, which is in the land of Canaan. After he made this request, he acknowledged that he had buried Rachel (wife of Jacob and mother of Joseph) near Bethlehem and not in the Cave of Machpelah.

Rashi describes Jacob's thoughts as he recounted his burial of Rachel: "And although I trouble you to carry me to be buried in the land of Canaan, and I did not do so for your mother, for she died near Bethlehem...and I did not even carry her to Bethlehem to bring her into the land of Canaan. And I know that you have a complaint in your heart against me. However, know that by the word of God did I bury her there, so that she would aid her children when Nevuzaradan would exile them and they would pass by there; then would Rachel come out upon her grave, crying and requesting mercy for them, as it is stated:[74] 'A voice is heard in Ramah...' And the Holy One Blessed be He answers her, 'There is a reward for your work, and your children will return to their own border' " (Jeremiah 31:16).

In the discourse from which the excerpt below is taken, the Rebbe expounds on *Rashi*'s opinion. He explains that Rachel actually desired to be buried in Bethlehem – not in the Cave of Machpelah – in order to assist her children by praying for them in their time of trouble. By being buried there, she missed out on the tremendous privilege of being

---

74   *Rashi*, Genesis 48:7

buried in the Cave of Machpelah. However, she was willing to make the sacrifice in order to help her children.

The Rebbe discusses the difference between men's and women's observance of the *mitzvot*. A man is obligated to do all of the *mitzvot*. On the other hand, because of her many obligations in the role of *akeret habayit* (the foundation of the Jewish home), the Jewish woman is relieved of the obligation to do many of the *mitzvot*. Though she may feel that she is missing out on the holiness of the *mitzvot* she is not obligated to perform, she gives up this opportunity in order to fulfill the needs of her family. God greatly appreciates and rewards this sacrifice, as we see from the promise that He made to Rachel as a reward for the sacrifice that she made: He promised that He will listen to her prayer, and that in her merit, her children will eventually return to their land.

The Rebbe writes:
Likkutei Sichot vol. 30, pp. 238-240

The fact that Jacob buried Rachel on the roadside "by the word of God...that she would be of aid to her children..." does not mean that Rachel was disadvantaged in order to benefit her children. On the contrary, since this was for the salvation of Rachel's children, it was for the benefit and happiness of Rachel. Therefore, Rachel herself would certainly have agreed to this, and would have requested it.

It is possible that this was *Rashi*'s intent in quoting the verse, "And the Holy One Blessed be He answers her, 'There is a reward for your work.' " This verse does not mention any work that Rachel did. However, *Rashi* was referring to the very fact that she was buried on the roadside, which was in order "that she would be of aid to her children."

Furthermore, the fact that God commanded Jacob to bury her there was because this was the will and desire of Rachel. To express this idea in different words: it was specifically Rachel's request for mercy that had the power to elicit the promise that "your children will return to their own border," in the merit of this "action," i.e., that she was prepared to relinquish the advantage of burial in the Cave of Machpelah in order "that she would be of aid to her children."

This quality that we find in Rachel — the <u>willingness to relinquish</u> her own advantage (to be buried together with Jacob, our patriarch, in the Cave of Machpelah) in order "that she would be of aid to her children" — is the fundamental quality that is found in every proper Jewish woman, whose role is to be the *akeret habayit*.

The explanation of the matter is:

Although the general principle of "I was created in order to serve my Master" is equally applicable to men and women, nevertheless there is a difference between men and women with regard to this principle. The main type of service of God of a man is studying Torah, prayer, and fulfillment of all of the commandments, which also includes (since he must be involved in worldly matters and earning a livelihood) his service of "In all your ways, know Him,"[75] and "All of your actions should be for the sake of Heaven."[76] In contrast, women are exempt from positive commandments that may be fulfilled only at specific times, and from the obligation to study Torah, since they must be involved with homemaking.

Perhaps it can be said that in this is seen the special virtue of women. Men's service of God is done mainly in a way that is visible, and therefore this type of service can engender a feeling of satisfaction ("content with his lot"), which can lead to a feeling of self-importance — at least in a very subtle way. This is not the case with women.

This distinction can help explain the different aspects of lineage. The essence and general characteristic of being a Jew

---

75 Proverbs 3:6, [*Artscroll Tanach*, Mesorah Publications, Ltd., Brooklyn, New York, 2003]

76 *Pirkei Avot* 2:12

depends specifically on the mother, because someone who is born to a Jewish mother is a Jew even if the father is not a Jew. However, the details and differences among Jews — *Kohen, Levi, Yisrael* — depend on the father's family.

A person's being a Jew depends on his being truly a part of God above, beyond divisions into specific categories, whereas the categories of *Kohen, Levi,* and *Yisrael* are different levels in the revelation of holiness, and this depends on the man whose service of God involves revealed aspects of holiness.

This was Jacob's intent when he said to Joseph, "And although I trouble you to carry me to be buried in Canaan, and I did not do so for your mother..."[77] This statement illustrates the difference between Jacob and Rachel. Because of the manner of Jacob's service, he had to be buried in the Cave of Machpelah together with the rest of the patriarchs — in a situation and location of revealed holiness.

The special virtue of Rachel — the mainstay of the home, the *akeret habayit* — was that she relinquished the completeness and merit that she could have had by being buried in the Cave of Machpelah in order "that she would be of aid to her children." This aid was in particular to the children that would live several generations later, children who would be in such an undesirable situation that they incurred the punishment of exile. For these children that sinned and were exiled, our matriarch Rachel relinquished the merit of being buried in the Cave of Machpelah together with our patriarch Jacob for thousands of years, in order that through this she would be able to be "of aid to her children."

This is the reason that she elicited the promise of "your children shall return to their own border" — she relinquished her own merit for the sake of these children because of the essential connection between her and them, in whatever situation they may be. This evokes from Above "measure for

---

77 [*Rashi*, Genesis 48:7]

measure," so that despite the apparent situation of the children for which they incurred the punishment of exile, God promised, "Your children shall return to their own border." Since they are His children, they will certainly return to their border with the true and complete redemption, may it be speedily in our days.

STUDY QUESTIONS:

1. What was Rachel's reason for being buried in Bethlehem rather than with the other Patriarchs and Matriarch in the Cave of Machpelah?

2. According to Rashi, what did Rachel do to deserve a reward from God?

3. What quality of Rachel is found in every proper Jewish woman?

4. Why might a man's service of God result in a feeling of self-importance, but a woman's service would not?

5. Whose service of God is done in a more revealed way – a man's or a woman's, and how is this expressed in
   i. The different aspects of lineage – Jew or non-Jew; Kohen Levi, or Yisrael?
   ii. The different types of burial place of Jacob and of Rachel?

6. For what type of descendants did Rachel pray for mercy?

7. How is Rachel's reward connected with her unconditional connection with her descendants?

Parashat Shemot

THE HEROIC JEWISH WOMEN IN EGYPT
SET AN EXAMPLE FOR US

Parashat Shemot describes the bitter slavery and persecution that the Jews suffered in Egypt. One of the harshest decrees of Pharaoh, king of Egypt, was that all Jewish newborn baby boys be killed. The Jewish midwives, Yocheved and Miriam, courageously defied Pharaoh's decree and kept the baby boys alive. Still, many Jews were discouraged by the decree, and husbands separated from their wives so that they would not have to face the terrible test of what to do if they would give birth to a boy. Miriam's parents, Amram and Yocheved, were among those who separated, but reunited with Miriam's encouragement. As a result, Moses, the leader of the Jews, was soon born, and eventually led them out of the slavery of Egypt to their redemption.

In this letter, dated the seventh of Adar, the birthday of Moses, the Rebbe addresses young women who are students in a seminary. He tells them how the heroism of Yocheved and Miriam made the birth of Moses possible. Similarly, the women of our generation have the merit and responsibility to raise the generation of the future redemption, and to do everything possible to hasten the arrival of the redeemer. The Rebbe urges the students to make their utmost effort to internalize the knowledge and fear of God which the seminary teaches them.

The Rebbe writes:
Likkutei Sichot vol.11, p.191

On this day, the birthday of Moses, it is certainly worthwhile to contemplate the fact that the birth, rescue, and education of the redeemer of Israel came about through the dedication of two Jewish women, a mother and a daughter: Yocheved, his mother, and Miriam, his sister. Pharaoh's decrees made the slavery extremely difficult, causing depression and marital separation even among the towering figures of the generation. However, even at this difficult time, these two women, the mother and daughter who were the Jewish midwives, were not discouraged. On the contrary, they continued their work with actual self-sacrifice, saving the baby boys, and in the severest part of the exile, they raised the generation of the redemption. Their determination and courage inspired not only the women, but also the men. They merited that their efforts would bring the redeemer of Israel to take the Jews out from slavery to redemption.

This same idea is applicable in the final generations of this bitter exile, and particularly in our generation. The same task and the same responsibility and merit that was the lot of the women in the first exile also belongs to the women of this final exile, as the Previous Rebbe frequently emphasized both in writing and orally. In this auspicious year, the 150th anniversary of the passing of the Alter Rebbe, the author of the *Tanya* and the [Alter Rebbe's] *Shulchan Aruch*, and the founder of the Chabad movement, its doctrines and way of life, we should recall and be impressed by the great influence of the Alter Rebbe's mother, Rebbetzin Rivkah, on his education, as described at length in the memoirs of the Previous Rebbe.

In keeping with his characteristic of putting words into action, for the action is the main thing, the Previous Rebbe not only talked about these concepts but actually established a network of schools and seminaries named "Bais Rivkah" in our Holy Land and in the Diaspora in which to educate Jewish girls in the spirit of Yocheved and Miriam.

Therefore, I hope from the depths of my heart that the students of this seminary will recognize their great responsibility and merit, and utilize all of their strength to internalize this spirit – the spirit of knowledge and fear of God – that the seminary wishes to impart to them. Since the students will become teachers and guides of the Jewish people, mothers of children and each one an *akeret habayit*, any increase in their education and knowledge is multiplied many times over in the students and in the homes that they will establish in honor and glory. All efforts and exertion toward this goal are worthwhile.

May God send His blessings to all of you for success in your diligent study and proper conduct. The blessing should be fulfilled in each and every one of you, that "Our sister, may you come to be thousands of myriads…" [78]

STUDY QUESTIONS:

1. How did Pharaoh's decrees affect Jewish family life in Egypt?

2. What courageous act did Yocheved and Miriam do during the time of Pharaoh's decrees?

3. What special result occurred due to Yocheved's and Miriam's heroism?

4. What is the relevance of Yocheved's and Miriam's actions for the women of today?

---

78 [Genesis 24:60, *Artscroll Tanach*, Mesorah Publications, Ltd., Brooklyn, New York, 2003]

5. Why is it so important that the students of the
    seminary internalize the spirit of knowledge and fear
    of God that the seminary imparts to them?

Parashat Va'eira

THE MERIT OF THE WOMEN
BRINGS THE REDEMPTION

At the end of the previous Torah portion, *Parashat Shemot*, the slavery and suffering in Egypt reached their peak of intensity. In the beginning of *Parashat Va'eira*, God notified Moses that the redemption was finally at hand. He said, "Moreover, I have heard the groan of the Children of Israel whom Egypt enslaves and I have remembered My covenant."[79] God then instructed Moses to inform the Jews that He will take them out of Egypt, and told him in detail about the imminent redemption.

The following selection is an excerpt from a discourse that the Rebbe delivered on the anniversary of the passing of his wife, Rebbetzin Chaya Mushka. In this excerpt, the Rebbe mentions the statement of the sages that it was in the merit of the righteous women of that generation that the Jews were redeemed from Egypt. He then proceeds to emphasize the privilege and duty of the women of the present generation to help bring about the future redemption.

The Rebbe writes:
Sefer HaSichot 5752, p. 354

Regarding the redemption from Egypt, the sages say,[80] "In the merit of the righteous women of that generation, the Jews were redeemed from Egypt." Similarly, the future

---

79   Exodus 6:5, [*Artscroll Tanach*, Mesorah Publications, Ltd., Brooklyn, New York, 2003]
80   *Sotah* 11b

redemption (about which the verse says,[81] "As in the days when you left the land of Egypt I will show it [Israel] wonders.") will take place in the merit of the righteous women of the generation that precedes the redemption. As our sages say, "A generation is redeemed only in the merit of the righteous women of that generation." In particular, the relevance of this statement of the sages to our generation is explained in the writings of Rabbi Yitzchak Luria, of blessed memory, who wrote that the final generation of the exile is a reincarnation of the generation that went out of Egypt.

The unique status of our generation is one of the reasons for the special effort that the Previous Rebbe made in the education and guidance of Jewish women and girls. This effort applied to all areas of Judaism, the Torah and its commandments, including the study of *Chassidut* and the dissemination of its teachings. Because our generation is the final generation of the exile and the first generation of the redemption, the Godly service of Jewish women and girls is especially important, for the redemption comes in their merit.

STUDY QUESTIONS:

1.   In whose merit were the Jews redeemed from Egypt?

2.   How did our sages generalize this principle for succeeding generations?

3.   According to Rabbi Yitzchak Luria, what is the connection between the generation that left Egypt and the final generation of the exile?

4.   What efforts did the Previous Rebbe make in connection with the education of Jewish women and girls?

---

81   Micah 7:15, [*Artscroll Tanach,* Mesorah Publications, Ltd., Brooklyn, New York, 2003]

5.   What is the special status of the current generation?

Parashat Bo

EDUCATION OF JEWISH CHILDREN

Parashat Bo describes the exodus of the Jewish nation from Egypt. After the Jews left Egypt, they began their journey through the desert. This journey brought them to Mount Sinai, where they received the Torah, and it ultimately brought them to the Land of Israel.

The following selection is a letter that the Rebbe wrote to participants in a convention of N'shei uB'nos Chabad, a worldwide organization of Lubavitch women. In this letter, the Rebbe points out that the purpose of the redemption from Egypt was to receive the Torah at Mount Sinai. Even when the Jews were still in Egypt, the Jewish women were raising and educating their children to be prepared to receive the Torah. In particular, they taught their children to readily accept and obey whatever commandments God gave them. Similarly, in all generations, women have a crucial role in the education of children – of their own children and also of Jewish children in general.

The Rebbe writes:
Likkutei Sichot vol. 12, pp. 170-171

Recently, the subject of *chinuch* (Torah education of children) has been discussed on many occasions, and in connection with this — the special capacities, merit, and responsibility that women have in this vital matter.

Since the convention is taking place in the days of *Sefirah*, this time also has a special relevance for women regarding the topic of *chinuch*.

The days of *Sefirah* connect the Festival of the Liberation from Egypt — Pesach — with the Festival of the Giving of the Torah — Shavuot. This underscores the fact that the purpose of the liberation from slavery in Egypt was to receive the Torah. As God told Moses at the outset — when he will lead the Jews out of Egypt, they will receive the Torah at Mount Sinai: "When you take the people out of Egypt, you will serve God on this mountain."[82] This connection emphasizes that true freedom (Pesach is referred to as the time of our freedom) is achieved only through Torah (engraved on the stone tablets[83]).

In both events — the liberation from Egypt and the giving of the Torah — Jewish women had a very important share. Our sages tell us that it was in the merit of the righteous women that the Jews were freed from Egypt. In addition, as a preparation for receiving the Torah, God commanded Moses to address the women ("the house of Jacob ") first, and only thereafter, the men ("sons of Israel").

The meaning of Torah (which is grammatically related to the Hebrew word that means "teaching") is that it teaches a Jew how to conduct his daily life, from childhood through old age. This is what *chinuch* is all about.

In those days in Egypt, it was mainly thanks to the Jewish women and mothers that a new generation was brought up, which rose to the high spiritual level of receiving the Torah with *na'aseh v'nishma* [unconditional acceptance — doing first and understanding later]. Similarly in all times, and particularly in the present time, Jewish women and mothers have a very great share in the education of the children — their own as well as that of the others in their surroundings.

---

82 [Exodus 3:12, *Artscroll Tanach*, Mesorah Publications, Ltd., Brooklyn, New York, 2003]

83 [The letters of Torah were engraved (*charut*) on the stone tablets that God gave to Moses. The word *charut* is spelled with the same consonants as the word *cherut*, which means freedom. Thus, Torah is connected with freedom.]

Therefore, I hope and am certain that the convention will take advantage of this occasion to deal with the subject of *chinuch*, and the ways to strengthen and promote *chinuch*. This strengthening should be done both <u>quantitatively</u> — drawing in even more children to receive a Torah education — as well as <u>qualitatively</u> — giving an education that is Torah-true to the fullest measure. This Torah-true education should be expressed in a strong attachment and devotion to the Torah, <u>the Torah of life</u>, and to its *mitzvot*, about which the Torah says, "You shall live according to them." They are the very life of a Jew.

May God bless the convention with success, that it should fulfill all of its expectations, and more, both spiritually and materially.

<u>STUDY QUESTIONS:</u>

1. What was the immediate goal of the Jews' liberation from slavery in Egypt?

2. What can we learn from the fact that these pairs of words have similar meanings in Hebrew?
    i.   "Freedom" and "Engraved"?
    ii. "Torah" and "Teaching"?

3. What were the special roles of women in
    i.   The liberation from Egypt?
    ii. The giving of the Torah?

4. To which high spiritual level did the Jewish women in Egypt raise their children?

5.   In the present time, how can Jewish women promote the education of Jewish children?

Parashat Beshalach

A MOTHER'S JOY
AT THE RESCUE OF HER CHILDREN

Parashat Beshalach describes how Pharaoh and his Egyptian army pursued the Jewish people after they left Egypt. When the Jews got to the Sea of Reeds they were trapped – the sea was in front of them and the Egyptian army was behind them. Miraculously, God split the sea, making a path of dry land in the middle for the Jews to walk through. Undeterred, the Egyptians chased after the Jews, following them into the sea along this path. But God closed the path, drowning them and ending their pursuit. When the Jews made it safely across, they sang songs of thanks to God. The men sang a song led by Moses, and the women, using musical instruments, sang one led by Miriam. From this we see, as explained in the discourse below, that the women sang with greater joy than the men.

The Rebbe explains that the reason for the women's great joy was that Pharaoh's cruel decrees against the Jews were more painful for the women than they were for the men. Therefore, their joy at being liberated from those decrees was greater.

In the present time, the evil inclination influences us in ways analogous to Pharaoh's decrees. One attitude it promotes is that if parents want their child to be able to earn a livelihood when he grows up, they must immerse him in the secular culture. This attitude is analogous to Pharaoh's decree of throwing the baby boys into the river.

It is the mother who is most closely involved in the education of the children. Therefore, it is she who has the biggest struggle with the evil inclination's attitude that the child's education should be primarily secular. However, she must realize that for a Jew the only way to earn a livelihood is to be connected to God. When she finds the strength to educate her children according to Torah – which shows them how to be strongly connected to God – then she will derive true joy from her children, and her home will be blessed bountifully.

The Rebbe writes:

Likkutei Sichot[84] vol. 1, pp. 139-144

In a discourse[85] delivered twenty years ago, on the final day of Pesach 5698 [1938], the Rebbe, my father-in-law (the Previous Rebbe), discussed the *haftarah*[86] of this Shabbat.

At the time, he quoted his great-grandfather, the Tzemach Tzedek, who had said that his grandfather, the Alter Rebbe, once asked the question: Why is the *haftarah* of Shabbat *Shira* — "And Deborah sang"[87] — the song of a woman, and not the song of King David — which is the *haftarah* of the seventh day of Pesach? In *Parashat Beshalach* there is a song of men — "Then sang Moses..."[88] as well as a song of women — "Miriam took the drum in her hand and all the women went forth...with drums and with dances; and Miriam spoke up to them, 'Sing to God, for He is gloriously sublime...' "[89] Why then is the *haftarah* specifically the song of a woman, "And Deborah sang?"

The Alter Rebbe related a lengthy story regarding this (published in the above-mentioned discourse), and

---

84 Note: The translation of this discourse and accompanying references is based on *Likkutei Sichot*, vol. 2, pp. 62-71, Kehot Publication Society, 1983.
85 *Likkutei Diburim*, Likut 38
86 [The *haftarah* is a selection from the Prophets that is read after the Torah reading on Shabbat, and on Jewish festivals and fast days.]
87 Judges Chapter 5
88 Exodus Chapter 15
89 Exodus 15:20–21, *Artscroll Tanach*, [Mesorah Publications, Ltd., Brooklyn, New York, 2003]

concluded: when the Jews left Egypt, passed through dry land in the midst of the sea, and then offered a song, the women sang too. But the women did so "with drums and with dances," with joy. That is why the *haftarah* of Shabbat *Shirah* [literally, "Sabbath of Song"[90]] is "And Deborah sang."

This explanation is difficult to understand. Why, indeed, was the song of Moses and the children of Israel, i. e., the men, less joyous than that of Miriam and all of the women? In the plain sense, the reason is that it is impossible to sense the same joy in an accomplishment attained without effort and agony as when there is great exertion and the experience of difficult struggles. "The reward is commensurate to the pain":[91] the greater the effort and agony, the greater the joy that comes afterward.

When the Jewish people witnessed the drowning of the Egyptians and their own complete redemption from the Egyptian exile, they sang a song. But Moses and all the men could not feel at that time as intense a joy as did Miriam and all the women.

The most difficult period of the Egyptian exile, and the harshest decrees, occurred after the birth of Miriam. The most terrible decree of all was that "Every son that will be born — into the river shall you throw him!"[92]

All preceding hardships, the hard labor "with mortar and with bricks, and with every labor of the field; all their labors that they performed with them were with crushing harshness,"[93] were of no comparison to the decree of casting newborn babies into the river.

---

90   [This is a special name given to the Shabbat on which *Parashat Beshalach* is read.]
91   *Pirkei Avot* 5:21
92   Exodus 1:22
93   Exodus 1:13

Moreover, as our Sages relate,[94] this was followed by the decree that Pharaoh should bathe in the blood of the Jewish children.

Such things affect a mother much more than a father. Therefore, when the Jewish people were set free from Pharaoh and his decrees, the joy of the Jewish women was much greater than that of the men.

All narratives of the Torah offer instruction for every generation, up to our own. This includes the story of the exodus from Egypt and the song with the joy demonstrated by the drums and dances of Miriam and the Jewish women.

An allusion to this affect appears in Scripture itself, where it is stated "and <u>all</u> the women went forth <u>after</u> her"[95] — i.e., all Jewish women to the end of time follow Miriam and say "Sing unto God, for He is gloriously sublime, having hurled horse with its rider into the sea."[96]

Godliness and holiness are gloriously sublime; there can be nothing higher. All things contrary to holiness, which oppose holiness — signified by the horse and the rider — are "hurled into the sea," that is, hurled with power, to the very depths of the sea, lower than which there is nothing.

It was already discussed at an earlier occasion that the significance of the decree of "Every son that will be born — into the river shall you throw him!" is relevant to every generation and every country — including our own time and place.

The Jewish way of life is to educate the child with Torah and *mitzvot* beginning right after birth. But as soon as a Jewish child is born, Pharaoh, king of Egypt — that is, the dominant trend of society — comes and argues: a boy has been born, who in due time will marry and have to provide

---

94   *Shemot Rabba* 1:34
95   Exodus 15:20
96   Exodus 15:21

for his household. Thus, one must "throw him into the river" which provides a livelihood — analogous to the Nile River which was responsible for all of the food and sustenance of Egypt — from childhood on, to become immersed and drowned in that river.

But what will become of Torah and *mitzvot*? "Pharaoh" answers that there is a Sunday. On Sunday, the banks are closed, businesses are shut, and so forth. Saturday night the child must be taken to the movies and similar places. The next morning, however, as the parents want to sleep until noon, it doesn't bother them if the child goes to Sunday school to study not only songs and dancing, but even Hebrew and Chumash. This allows the parents to sleep peacefully and to be deeply submerged in sleep spiritually.

Afterwards, about one o'clock in the afternoon, the child will be nourished with television, movies and baseball — with the Nile River, which in their view provides sustenance.

They do this instead of what one must do — to bond the child from his very infancy to God, who sustains the entire world in His goodness with grace, kindness, and compassion in an honorable and peaceful way. This bond alone — connecting oneself with God — is the Jew's only channel for sustenance. Even if the laws of the Nile River may determine the livelihood of the gentiles, of Israel, however, it is said, "But you <u>who cling</u> unto the Eternal, your God — you are all <u>alive</u> today."[97] Their life derives from this bond of cleaving unto God — it is through <u>this</u> that they live, and through this they also have their livelihood — for "He Who gives life also gives sustenance" — for himself, his wife, and children.

Instead of following this path, they take their children and throw them into the river, which tears them away, not only from spiritual reality, but also from life itself. For, as said, the

---

97   Deuteronomy 4:4

sole channel for the life and livelihood of a Jew is his bond with God.

In the Egyptian exile, which preceded the giving of the Torah, none of the earlier hardships were as terrible as the decree of, "Every son that will be born — into the river shall you throw him!" It is the same with the present exile. None of the decrees that the evil inclination makes for adults is as terrible as the one against their own children.

One must not be influenced by "Pharaoh" or "good friends" like the next-door neighbor who argues, "How can you send your child to a *cheder* or to a yeshiva to be taught a Torah that is some 3,500 years old, a Torah given in a desolate desert and in a time when there was no radio and no telephone, and not even a morning paper after *Modeh Ani*[98] to start the day! In those primitive days, it was all right to pursue an education like that. Today, however, in the twentieth century endowed with progress and culture, we cannot be old-fashioned!"

Moreover, Pharaoh will sometimes don a mantle of holiness and argue, "Surely you would like your child to contribute large sums to charity in general and to yeshivas in particular. Then you must see to it that he be wealthy, and therefore cast him into the river of sustenance. Make him be like all the Johns and Michaels who are not involved with Divine service, and then there is a chance that he will contribute money to yeshivas and *chadarim*! In reality, however, Pharaoh is the only one to profit from this. The Jewish nation gains nothing.

One must be aware of the truth that this decree comes from the same Pharaoh. He realizes that any demand to commit a transgression will not be obeyed. Therefore, he disguises himself in a silken caftan [a saint's clothing, as it

---

98 [*Modeh Ani* is a short prayer that is said immediately upon awakening in the morning.]

were] and claims to have a large yeshiva for which he needs funds. Children should therefore be sent to public schools and Sunday schools, and this will enable them to build large yeshivas for — <u>angels</u>.

One must realize that this advice originates from Pharaoh, the "crafty one," who says, "Come let us outsmart them, lest they become numerous"[99] (however, the fact is that they will indeed become numerous and grow!) — the Pharaoh who desires that there remain no remnant or residue, Heaven forbid, of Judaism and Jewish souls, and thus also not of Jewish bodies.

One must react with Jewish determination to annul the edict. Stop worrying about the children's careers when they are five, seven, thirteen, or eighteen years old, and have faith and trust in the Almighty. For, "Many are the thoughts in the heart of man" (and these are of no avail precisely because they are many: multifariousness as opposed to the oneness of the ultimate One of the universe), "but the plan of God, it endures"[100] (the original Hebrew of "it" in the singular tense). The Almighty controls not only the heavens but also this very earth, in which she lives with her husband and children.

When keeping this in mind, she will not be influenced by her neighbor, but on the contrary, she will influence the neighbor to save her children from Pharaoh's hands as well. Tens of thousands of children will thus be raised to march towards our righteous *Mashiach*, speedily in our own days.

In the time of Moses and Miriam, when we were redeemed from Pharaoh, the joy of the women was much greater than the joy of the men, because the mothers' agony over the harsh edicts was also more profound than that of the fathers.' It is the same today: "Edicts of Pharaoh," as well as

---

99   Exodus 1:10
100   Proverbs 19:21

the joy that comes from overcoming them, are felt more profoundly by Jewish women.

A man is not at home for the major part of the day. Even during the time that he is home, he is not as involved with the education of the children as the mother. In contrast, the Jewish woman is constantly locked in battle with Pharaoh in all his disguises and ruses of good friendship. Thus, it is she who is assured to be victorious and to achieve that "the Eternal (i.e., Torah and Judaism) is most exalted; the horse and its rider (the opposing side), He has hurled into the sea." This is achieved through joy, with drums and with dances, thus leading into the next Torah portion, Yitro, the Torah portion of the receiving of the Torah, because now one is able to state, "Our children shall be our guarantors."[101]

Thus, we can understand a passage in *Midrash Tanchuma*[102] relating to an apparent difficulty in the verse, "Miriam spoke up *lahem* (to them)"[103]: The context suggests that Miriam spoke up to the *women*; thus, it should say *lahen* in the feminine gender and not *lahem* in the masculine gender!

The *Midrash* relates that when the Israelites crossed the sea and sang the song, the angels, too, wanted to offer a song. The Almighty then said to the angels, "Israel shall sing first, and only then will you sing."

The *Midrash* thus explains the expression "*az yashir* Moshe" — "then sang Moses." It does not say *shar* (the proper grammatical form for the past tense, third person singular) but *yashir* (future tense) — indicating a command of God: "(first) Moses shall sing with the children of Israel, and the angels only thereafter."

When Miriam and the women were about to offer their song, the angels argued once more: "We ceded priority to

---

101 *Shir Hashirim Rabba* I:4:1
102 *Tanchuma-Kadum, Bereishit* 13; See also *Shemot Rabba* 23:7
103 Exodus 15:21

Moses and Israel, but now we want to sing <u>before</u> the women." According to one authority in the *Midrash*, the angels did get their wish, but according to a second opinion, the song of the women, too, preceded the song of the angels.

However, even according to the opinion that the angels did not wait for the women, they could not offer their song until Miriam granted them permission. This explains why it says, "Miriam spoke up *lahem*" — masculine gender: that is, *lahem* refers to the angels, to whom Miriam granted permission to offer their song.

From this passage, we can see the great significance of the women's song. Its impact was felt not only in this physical world but also in the supernal, spiritual realms. Their song took precedence and was superior to that of the angels.

All the above offers clear guidance for every Jew. There is no reason to be afraid, neither of Pharaoh, nor of the Nile, nor of all harsh decrees. When fortified with authentic Jewish vigor, one can be in Egypt even when there is a Pharaoh with all kinds of decrees, and still have one's children unaffected — he will guide his children in the way of Torah, which is the way that brings them life, not only life in the World to Come, but also literally life in this world.

He will guide the children along the path that will cause them to say, "This is my God and I will glorify Him, <u>my father's</u> God and I will exalt Him;"[104] for they shall follow the path of their parents. Surely, this is authentic joy from children.

Then this will lead — as the song continues – to, "You will bring them and plant them on the Mountain of Your heritage,"[105] i.e., to merit the building of the third, eternal *Beit Hamikdash*, speedily in our own days.

---

104 Exodus 15:2
105 Exodus 15:17

Moreover, as stated in the *Gemara*,[106] "You can learn of God's love for Israel from the fact that the Almighty did not wait for the fulfillment of 'You will bring them and plant them on the Mount of Your heritage,' which refers to the *Beit Hamikdash* in Jerusalem, but when they were still in the desert, God already said, 'They shall make a Sanctuary for Me — so that I may dwell among them.[107]'"

It is the same now, in these few days remaining before the coming of *Mashiach*. Remaining unaffected by all sorts of decrees, and raising "seed blessed by the Eternal,"[108] brings about, "They shall make a Sanctuary for Me — so that I may dwell among them." That is, the Almighty will dwell in every Jewish home. Since God dwells there, it is inevitable that there will also be bountiful sustenance, plentiful health, and true joy from children and grandchildren, for many good days and years.

STUDY QUESTIONS:

1. In what way was the women's song after crossing the Red Sea superior to the men's song?

2. What circumstances in Egypt affected the women more severely than they affected the men?

3. What is the present day analog of Pharaoh's decree of throwing the baby boys into the river? What would "Pharaoh" wish to do to the Jewish children of today?

4. What is the present day analog of the Nile river?

---

106 *Ketubot* 62b
107 Exodus 25:8
108 Isaiah 61:9

5. What is wrong with the argument that children should go to public schools so that they would someday be able to donate large sums to charity?

6. What should a Jewish mother keep in mind so she will have the strength to resist "Pharaoh's" present day decrees?

7. What is the reward for standing strong against "Pharaoh's" decrees?

Parashat Yitro

THE WOMEN WERE FIRST
AT THE GIVING OF THE TORAH

Parashat Yitro describes the giving of the Torah from God to the Jewish people, beginning with the events leading up to that momentous occasion. At the very start of those preparations, God told Moses, "So shall you say to the House of Jacob and relate to the Children of Israel."[109] In this verse, the "House of Jacob" is understood as referring to the women, the "Children of Israel" the men. Thus, by mentioning the women before the men, God instructed Moses to speak first to the women when conveying God's commandments.

The following selection is a letter that the Rebbe wrote to the graduating class of Bais Rivkah School. In this letter, the Rebbe points out that because God instructed Moses to address the women first, we know there is a particular merit and responsibility upon Jewish women to observe the commandments of the Torah. Also, as homemakers and mothers, they have the special role of transmitting the Torah to the next generation.

The Rebbe writes:
Likkutei Sichot vol. 22, pp. 294-295

Blessing and greeting!

I was pleased to receive notification concerning the graduation.

---

109 Exodus 19:3, *Artscroll Tanach*, Mesorah Publications, Ltd., Brooklyn, New York, 2003

You are certainly aware of an idea that has been mentioned several times: Any "conclusion" connected with a pure and holy Torah education is actually a preparation for, and an ascent to, a higher level — higher quantitatively as well as qualitatively.

May God grant that the graduation occur in a good and auspicious time, and may God give each of you success in fulfilling your heart 's desires for the good, and in continually progressing to higher levels in learning Torah, observance of its commandments, and in proper conduct.

These ideas are particularly applicable in this special time, the days of *Sefirah*, which are days of preparation for, and anticipation of, receiving the Torah on the holiday of Shavuot, the time of the giving of our Torah. It is well known what our Sages tell us — that when God prepared to give the Torah to His nation Israel, He commanded Moses to speak first with the women and afterwards with the men. This interpretation is hinted at in the verse, "So shall you say to the House of Jacob (the women) and relate to the Children of Israel (the men)." Because of this, Jewish women and girls have a special merit and responsibility regarding the receiving of the Torah — to observe its commandments and to transmit it from one generation to the next. It is understood that this is connected with the role of every Jewish daughter as *akeret habayit* and mother of children. For this role, an extra great preparation is required, and if it is not done now, then when?

STUDY QUESTIONS:

1.   What is the proper attitude toward reaching a milestone in Torah study?

2.   What good resolutions should one make when reaching such a milestone?

3.   To whom did God speak first when He was preparing to give the Torah to the Jews?

4.   What special merit and responsibility do Jewish women have as a result of this?

5.   How soon should a Jewish woman begin preparing for these roles?

Parashat Mishpatim

THE SHABBAT CANDLES
BRING LIGHT TO THE WHOLE FAMILY

Parashat Mishpatim mentions the commandment to observe Shabbat, the day of rest.

In the following selection, the Rebbe describes the special role that women play in the observance of Shabbat. It is the lighting of the candles, primarily done by women, that marks the beginning of Shabbat. The lighting of the Shabbat candles not only brings physical light to the home, but it also represents the ability that the Jewish woman has to illuminate her household with spiritual light. The Jewish woman has the ability, and indeed the obligation, to bring to her family a spiritual inspiration that extends from Shabbat into the rest of the week.

The Rebbe writes:
Likkutei Sichot vol. 2, p. 552

The first commandment that brings Shabbat into the home is lighting the Shabbat candles. This comes even before *Kabbalat Shabbat*[110] and *Kiddush*.[111] The thing with which Shabbat starts off is the illuminating of the Jewish home.

This commandment is one of the mitzvot that God has given mainly to women. They should illuminate the Jewish home, and through them the light comes to the entire family — husband, children, and siblings.

---

110 [*Kabbalat Shabbat* is the first of the Shabbat prayers.]
111 [*Kiddush*, in this context, is the prayer said at the beginning of the Friday night Shabbat meal.]

The Alter Rebbe says that the reason this commandment was given to women is that the woman is in the home most of the time, and she is occupied with providing for the needs of the home.

As mentioned earlier, Shabbat must influence and does influence all the days of the week. This is especially true with regard to the beginning of Shabbat — to lighting the candles. Jewish women have the power and the commandment to illuminate the home with Jewish light for the whole family and to draw this light from Shabbat into the rest of the week.

The *Zohar* states that the woman must light the candles with heartfelt joy. The same is true regarding the inner content of the commandment — illuminating the home. It must be done in a manner that is, and the light is, genuinely happy and full of feeling.

Everything that the Rebbes — beginning with the Baal Shem Tov, and continuing with the Alter Rebbe until the Previous Rebbe — demanded from their *Chassidim*, was with the desire that the *Chassidim*, both men and women, would in so doing lead the way for all Jews.

May God bless all of you and each of you individually, that you should show the way for all Jewish women to illuminate the Jewish home with heartfelt joy and feeling, to illuminate the day of Shabbat and to bring some of this light into the weekdays to make them holy also, and to do all of this with joy and gladness of heart.

STUDY QUESTIONS:

1.　　What is the first act that brings Shabbat into the home?

2.　　How does the woman's lighting the candles affect
　　　a. The rest of her family
　　　b. The rest of the week?

3.   What special power do Jewish women have to influence their family in connection with light?

4.   How should the woman feel when she lights the candles?

5.   What kind of influence should the woman have on other Jews regarding lighting Shabbat candles?

Parashat Terumah

MAKING ONE'S HOME
A DWELLING PLACE FOR GOD

In *Parashat Terumah*, God asks the Jewish people for donations of materials for construction of the *Mishkan*, the Sanctuary in which God's presence would dwell.

The following selection is an excerpt from a letter that the Rebbe wrote to a Lubavitch women's group. He explains that every Jewish home must be a holy place in which God's presence can dwell. As God has given women special capabilities to establish a truly Jewish home, it is the women who have the major role in accomplishing this objective.

The Rebbe writes:
Likkutei Sichot vol. 11, pp. 316-317

At this opportunity, I would like to underscore the tremendous merit and special capabilities that God has given to the women to establish the home in such a way that it will be a truly Jewish home, and to devote themselves to the upbringing of the children, in addition to their other *mitzvot*.

During these days and weeks, we read the portions in the Torah that are connected with setting up the *Mishkan*, the Sanctuary. They emphasize that the women were the first and most dedicated in this holy work.

The idea of building a sanctuary is applicable to every Jew, man or woman. It represents the establishment of one's own home, for every Jewish home must be a sanctuary to God. However, the major part of setting up this sanctuary belongs to the woman.

It is also explained in many places in the Gemara and *Zohar* that the woman's strengthening her observance of *tzniut* (modesty) is a way to assure health, income, and a lot of happiness — true happiness — from children and grandchildren. It is up to every individual to do this herself, and also to see to it that her good friends, relatives and acquaintances are also aware of the great capabilities that they have, and of the success connected with it.

May God help every one of you to act in these matters according to your full capabilities. Then God will certainly fulfill His promise to give health, income, and true happiness in a full measure.

STUDY QUESTIONS:

1. What is one of the special capabilities that God has given to Jewish women?

2. What was special about the Jewish women's approach to the building of the *Mishkan*?

3. What is the analog to the *Mishkan* in the life of each person?

4. When the woman strengthens herself in which mitzvah will she be assured of much happiness from children and grandchildren?

5. What should the woman make sure to bring to the awareness of her acquaintances?

Parashat Tetzaveh

BEAUTIFYING ONE'S SURROUNDINGS FOR GOD

Parashat Tetzaveh describes in detail the clothing that is to be worn by the *Kohen Gadol* and the other *kohanim* while they perform their service in the *Mishkan*, and later in the Holy Temple. In His instructions to Moses concerning their design, God said that the garments are to be made "for honor and for beauty."[112] Thus, the service performed by the *kohanim* in the *Mishkan* is meant to bring beauty to the *kohanim*, and thus to the Mishkan.

A basic principle in *Chassidut* is that God created and continuously maintains this physical world in order to have a "dwelling place" in this lowest of all worlds. We transform this world into such a dwelling place by carrying out God's commandments. In the following excerpt from a discourse, the Rebbe explains that women have a special role in making God's dwelling place in this world a beautiful one. In particular, just as it is the woman who physically beautifies a family's home, it is the woman who, by performing her special *mitzvot*, brings spiritual beauty to God's dwelling place in this world. Also, in the woman's role as educator of her young children, she imbues her children with a warmth and love for *mitzvot*, which they will in turn carry out in a beautiful way.

As described in the selection for *Parashat Terumah* (page 109), establishing one's own home based on the foundation of Torah and *mitzvot* is analogous to building a Temple in which God's presence can dwell. Therefore, the woman's role in

---

112 Exodus 28:2, 28:40

beautifying her home both spiritually and physically is analogous to the *kohen's* role in beautifying the Holy Temple.

The Rebbe writes:
Sefer haSichot 5752, pp. 356-357 (section 14)

We see in practical terms that in a home, the beauty of the home and its contents — both material and spiritual — depend mainly on the woman, the *akeret habayit*. As is known, the idea of beauty (and the power to create beauty) is found especially in a woman. The Talmud[113] mentions beauty in connection with women in several places — "A beautiful woman," "a beautiful and graceful bride," and even "A woman is only for beauty,"[114] i.e., spiritual beauty, which manifests itself in physical beauty.

It is possible to say this originates from the fact that in the service of making for God a "dwelling place in this lower world," a major part of the service consists of making it a "beautiful dwelling" with "beautiful utensils" and this depends on Jewish women and girls.

This idea is especially underscored in the three main *mitzvot* by which the entire Jewish nation is supported — lighting the candles of the holy Shabbat and *Yom Tov*, *kashrut* of food and drink, and family purity (the initials of the Hebrew words for these three *mitzvot* spell *hachen*, which means grace, attractiveness or beauty). These *mitzvot* cause it to be (besides a dwelling place for God in general) a "beautiful dwelling" with "beautiful utensils," permeated with the beauty, spiritual and physical, of *kashrut*, purity, and holiness.

Similarly, in the area of educating sons and daughters, which establishes the foundation of life for every person, we see in practical terms that it depends on the mother, most

---

113 *Berachot* 57b
114 *Taanit* 31a

particularly the education and training of young children. The younger the child, the more his education depends on the mother. She implants in them from the youngest age and onward the vitality and spirit of Judaism, and based on this foundation, sons and daughters are raised who are involved in the Torah and its *mitzvot*, with spiritual and physical completeness — in a beautiful and attractive way.

This means that besides the fact that the children will be involved in Torah and *mitzvot* in the ordinary way, the mother implants in them the delectability and warmth of observance of the *mitzvot*, with the gentleness and affection that is especially part of the nature of Jewish women and girls. Then, their involvement in Torah and *mitzvot* will be in a way that is <u>beautiful and good</u>, such that one can point to Him and say, "This is my God and I will beautify Him."

We see an example of this in the proper custom of Jewish mothers to sing to their very young children after laying them in their cradles, that the Torah is the best thing, the sweetest thing, the nicest thing, etc. This implants in the child — also when he grows up ("...also when he grows old it will not depart from him"[115]) — a deep affection and esteem for all matters of Torah and *mitzvot*.

STUDY QUESTIONS:

1. When the Talmud refers to the beauty of women, to what type of beauty does it refer?

2. What is an important way to augment God's dwelling place in this lower world?

3. The performance of which commandments brings a special beauty (spiritual and physical) to the Jewish home?

---

115 Proverbs 22:6

4.   What can a mother do to implant in her children an appreciation for the Torah and its commandments?

5.   What character attributes of Jewish women help them in influencing their children most effectively?

Parashat Ki Tisa

WOMEN'S SPECIAL ABILITY
TO EXPRESS FAITH THROUGH ACTION

Parashat Ki Tisa describes how some Jews constructed and worshiped a calf made of gold. The reason they made this Golden Calf was out of despair; Moses had not yet returned from the heights of Mount Sinai at the expected time. Assuming he would never come back, they hoped this Golden Calf would be their new intermediary between themselves and God. However, this act was considered by God to be a grievous sin, an act of idol worship, and they were punished.

In the following excerpt from a discourse, the Rebbe points out that the women refused to contribute to the construction of the Golden Calf. He explains how they were able to find the strength to refrain from this sin. Although every Jew has an unshakeable faith in God deep within the heart, women have a special ability to ensure that this faith is manifested in their actions. Therefore, when Jewish women are subject to spiritual challenges, such as building the Golden Calf, they are able to derive enough strength from this faith to do the right thing. Jewish women must make sure that they constantly utilize this faith to illuminate their lives and to overcome any spiritual obstacles that they may encounter.

The Rebbe writes:
Likkutei Sichot vol. 8, pp. 315-317

Rosh Chodesh[116] has a special connection with the Jewish nation in general, as we see from the text that the Men of the

---

116   [*Rosh Chodesh* is the first day of a Hebrew month.]

Great Assembly have established for the *Mussaf* prayer of *Rosh Chodesh*: "You have given the days of *Rosh Chodesh* to Your people." In addition, *Rosh Chodesh* has a special connection with Jewish women. This was given to them as a reward, as it is related in *Pirkei deRabbi Eliezer*, for the strong attachment the women displayed to God when the Jews were in the desert, despite the strong delusion that prevailed at that time. This actually took place after the Jews spent two hundred and ten years in enslavement to the nation of Egypt, a land that ruled over the entire world, and was completely permeated with the worthlessness of idol worship. Therefore, it need not be so puzzling, that coming into the desert even after all the miracles that the Jews saw and experienced, a few people would be misled and say about something that is not God, "This is your god, Israel."[117] Even when doing so, they considered this nothing more than a partner with God.

Nevertheless, *Pirkei deRabbi Eliezer* explains, even in that situation of trial and delusion that prevailed in the desert, the women refused to take part. They said that under no circumstances would they agree to participate in making or recognizing as a god a worthless object that has no power, for the only reliance, trust, and strength of the Jews is in God.

Therefore, God allocated a special reward to the Jewish women of all generations: their connection shall be "to observe the days of *Rosh Chodesh* even more than the men."[118] The connection of the men is expressed, for the most part, in the designated prayers and blessings of *Rosh Chodesh*, etc. Women have this additional observance of refraining from various types of work on the day of *Rosh Chodesh*.

This was given to them as a reward for all generations, as long as the eternal Jewish nation exists. Moreover, as *Pirkei deRabbi Eliezer* concludes, besides the above-mentioned eternal reward for the women in this world, they will be

---

117 Exodus 32:4
118 *Tur Orach Chaim* Chapter 417

given an additional reward in the future, after the coming of *Mashiach*: "Who satisfies your mouth with goodness, so that your youth is renewed like the eagle."[119] Their health will be (like the days of *Rosh Chodesh*) renewed and refreshed with youth, and they will be satiated with good in all matters. From this it is understood that this reward is not only because of the virtue of the women of that generation, who were able to withstand such a formidable trial that not all of the men withstood, but rather because this is an inborn virtue in all Jewish women of all generations. Therefore, this reward is given also to all women in all times until the coming of our righteous *Mashiach*, and even afterward.

Why, indeed, do women have this power and virtue even more than men? This can be understood according to that which is explained in various places, that the entire Jewish religion is based on faith, on pure belief in God. It is true that together with this, a Jew strives, as much as he is able, to understand God's greatness with his mind as well. However, first of all, and last of all, he has the pure feeling of faith, a feeling that cannot be shaken or disturbed by difficulties and trials, etc.

This very power and feeling is actually implanted in the heart of every Jew, men as well as women, because they are all sons of Abraham, Isaac, and Jacob, and daughters of Sarah, Rebecca, Rachel and Leah. However, it can occasionally happen that this feeling, although it remains complete and strong, becomes obscured and concealed. That is, because of various circumstances, its effect is not apparent in day-to-day life. In this detail, the woman has within herself a special strength not to allow this feeling to become hidden — not only does the feeling itself not, God forbid, become disturbed, but its effect on one's various activities also remains undisturbed.

---

119 Psalms 103:5, [*Artscroll Tanach*, Mesorah Publications, Ltd., Brooklyn, New York, 2003]

Therefore, we always find (even when the Jews are confronted with a trial) that they are labeled as "believers, children of believers" — and yet the effect of this feeling of faith did not have sufficient impact to prevent the men from contributing gold for the "calf" (a sin of idol worship), although deep down in their essence, the feeling of faith remained as strong as before. However, in women, the <u>effect</u> of this feeling of faith remained then in its full vigor, and with the greatest resoluteness they refused to give gold for the Golden Calf.

This illustrates, as mentioned earlier, the inborn attribute of all Jewish women in every <u>time</u> and generation — also in our generation, just as in the generations before and also after us, and including all of the daughters of Israel in every <u>place</u>.

Not only does the feeling of faith remain fully undisturbed and in its full strength, but the same strength of faith that is expressed in them permeates all their activities and is reflected in the various events of their day-to-day life — not to be affected by difficulties and interference from those who do not like them or who laugh at the Jewish holy conduct and so on. Rather, one goes firmly and proudly with the power of faith, which points the way and illuminates at all times of day, in all days of the week, in all weeks of the year, and in all the years of a person's life.

STUDY QUESTIONS:

1. Why might it not seem unreasonable that some people were attracted to idol worship when the Jews were in the desert?

2. Why do women have a special connection with Rosh Chodesh?

3. What do women do to observe their holiday of Rosh Chodesh?

4.   What can we learn from the fact that women of all
       generations are rewarded for the refusal of the women
       in the desert to participate in idol worship?

5.   What special character trait do women have that
       enables them to resist influences that are contrary to
       Torah?

Parashat Vayakhel

WOMEN'S ENTHUSIASM
FOR MAKING A DWELLING PLACE FOR GOD

In *Parashat Vayakhel*, Moses requested, according to God's instruction, contributions of the various materials necessary for the construction of the *Mishkan*, and the holy garments for the *kohanim*. The commentaries explain that the women contributed their jewelry for this purpose with extraordinary enthusiasm.[120] The Jewish women of that time did not always donate their jewelry so readily; they refused to contribute any toward the construction of the Golden Calf, as discussed in connection with *Parashat Ki Tisa* (page 115). Thus, the women were enthusiastic about donating their jewelry only for holy purposes.

The following selection is a letter that the Rebbe wrote to participants in a banquet for the Bais Rivkah girls' school. In this letter, the Rebbe explains the source of the women's enthusiasm about contributing toward the construction of the *Mishkan*: they understood that God's main goal is to have a dwelling place in this world. They also realized that they have a major role in fulfilling this goal, because as *akeret habayit*, the woman makes her own home a dwelling place for God's presence. The Rebbe stresses the vital importance of educating Jewish girls to feel as dedicated as those women were in making their own homes such a dwelling place.

---

120   See Ramban's commentary on Exodus 35:22.

The Rebbe writes:
Likkutei Sichot vol. 21, pp. 481-482

On the occasion of this wonderful event, I send my greeting and blessing to the guests and to all the participants and friends of Bais Rivkah, with the heartfelt wish that it should be very successful in all respects.

It is particularly relevant that the banquet takes place the day after the Shabbat of *Parashat Terumah*, the first of a series of Torah portions that discusses the setup of the Sanctuary and *Mishkan*. In connection with this, it is hinted in the Torah — and our Sages of blessed memory underscore this in detail — that when the women heard from Moses that God wants and requests,[121] "They shall make a Sanctuary for Me so that I may dwell among them" (we should make a holy place for Him, a dwelling place and a Sanctuary, and God's Presence will dwell among the Jews and in every Jew), the women responded with a fervor and inspiration that surpassed even that of the men, giving up for this holy purpose their precious jewelry, etc. The women understood that since God's principal intention is that "I may dwell among them" — that God's Presence shall dwell in every Jewish home — the women and daughters have a very great portion in this, since the entire conduct of the Jewish household depends in a large measure on the *akeret habayit*.

This provides a timely lesson and reminder for every one of us concerning the utmost importance of the Bais Rivkah institutions, where Jewish daughters are educated in the spirit of the righteous women who brought up the generation that was redeemed from Egypt, and who were the first to receive the Torah, and afterward the first who helped, with so much fervor and eagerness, to realize, "They shall make a Sanctuary for Me so that I may dwell among them."

---

121 [Exodus 25:8, *Artscroll Tanach*]

I am hopeful and certain that all the participants and friends of Bais Rivkah will enthusiastically respond to help ensure and strengthen the vitally important educational activity of this institution even more. In addition to the fact that doing so widens the channels through which to receive God's blessings for oneself and one's household (may they live) in everything they need materially and spiritually, it also hastens the time when the *Beit Hamikdash*, literally, will be rebuilt with the coming of our righteous *Mashiach*, very soon.

<u>STUDY QUESTIONS:</u>

1.   In what way was the women's contribution to the *Mishkan* greater than that of the men?

2.   How do we know that the Jewish home is similar to the *Mishkan*?

3.   What was the women's motivation for making such a special contribution to the building of the *Mishkan*?

4.   On whom does the conduct of the Jewish household largely depend?

5.   What are two types of benefits a person would receive if he supports the education of Jewish girls to follow the example of the women in the desert?

Parashat Pekudei

BRINGING HOLINESS INTO THE DESERT

Parashat Pekudei is the last of four *parashiot* that deal with the design and construction of the various parts of the *Mishkan*. This Torah portion in particular describes the completion of the construction of the parts of the *Mishkan*, and Moses' assembly of them for the first time, after which a cloud representing God's glory miraculously filled and covered the *Mishkan*.

The following section is an excerpt from a letter that the Rebbe wrote to the women and girls of Chabad. In this letter, the Rebbe points out that the *Mishkan*, a place of holiness, was built in the desert. A physical desert is an empty and dangerous place, and so is its spiritual counterpart, an environment whose ideas are empty of holiness.

The women had a leading role in the construction of the *Mishkan*, a place of holiness in the physical desert. Similarly, they must also assume a leading role in bringing holiness into environments that can be considered spiritual deserts.

The Rebbe writes:
Likkutei Sichot vol. 2, pp. 296-297

Even when Jews find themselves in a desert, they have the ability to establish a place of sanctity — a *Mishkan* — for God's Presence to dwell among the Jews in general, and within every Jew in particular.

Just as there is a physical desert, a wilderness where extreme climates and all kinds of threats prevail, there is also a <u>spiritual</u> desert where the most harmful spiritual ideas prevail. A spiritual desert may exist even in a land that is physically a blooming garden.

Our holy Torah teaches us that when we find ourselves in a spiritual desert, we can, and therefore <u>must</u>, establish a sanctuary, carrying it forward, walking in the footsteps [as it were] of God's Presence, until we reach the Divinely blessed Holy Land, and reach the true and complete redemption through the righteous *Mashiach*.

This is a lesson for *all* Jews, but especially for Jewish women, for as is known when it came to building the *Mishkan*, the women were the first to respond, even before the men.

In the spiritual desert of certain circles, where desolation and emptiness in matters of Judaism prevail, and all the more so with respect to a Chassidic way of life, women have the great and perpetual merit to be among the first to establish a *Mishkan* for the Divine Presence.

Special attention must be given to the very young children. For as we clearly see, when one raises a child properly from the earliest age and onward, one is guaranteed much more success and greater and better results.

STUDY QUESTIONS:

1.   What sort of effect should one have on one's environment, even if it seems as empty as a desert?

2.   What is the spiritual analog of a physical desert – what are its characteristics?

3.   How can one improve the environment in a spiritual desert?

4.   How do we know that women have a special role in improving the environment in spiritual deserts?

5.   Why is it especially important to teach very young
      children about Judaism?

Parashat Vayikra

DOING THE *MITZVOT*
IN THE MOST BEAUTIFUL WAY POSSIBLE

The concluding Torah portions in the Book of *Shemot* discuss the building of the *Mishkan*, a place where God's holiness would dwell in a revealed way. Directly following this, in the beginning of *Parashat Vayikra*, God tells of the rituals to be performed within that holy place. It is the first Torah portion that describes the laws of the ritual sacrifices in detail.

Some of the laws pertaining to ritual sacrifices concern *cheilev*, a type of fat found in animals that may be brought as a ritual sacrifice. The Torah tells us that *cheilev* may not be eaten. Also, the *cheilev* of animals brought as a ritual sacrifice must be entirely offered to God on the altar. As the verse says,[122] "…All *cheilev* is for God."

Although this verse is mentioned in the context of laws of ritual sacrifices, it is also interpreted to be a guiding principle in our service of God. The *cheilev* of an animal symbolizes the finest, choicest part of the animal. Just as we must offer all of the *cheilev* to God, we must also offer God the best of whatever we have. As Maimonides states,[123] "The law regarding anything that is done for the sake of God is that it should be done in the best and most beautiful way. If one builds a House of Prayer, it should be more beautiful than his home. One who gives food to a hungry person should give him from the best and sweetest food on his table. One who gives clothing to a needy person should give him from the

---

122 Leviticus 3:16
123 *Hilchot Issurei Hamizbeach* 7:1

nicest clothes he owns. One who designates some item from his belongings to be used for a holy purpose should designate from the nicest of his belongings. As the verse says, 'All *cheilev* is for God.' "

The following section is from a discourse that the Rebbe gave to an international convention of the Lubavitch Women's Organization. The Rebbe describes the extraordinary dedication that women exhibit in their performance of various *mitzvot* and discusses in detail their observance of some foremost examples of these: the *mitzvot* of preparation for Shabbat, giving charity, and learning Torah. He describes how women perform these *mitzvot*, and many others, with a special warmth that motivates them to do them in the most beautiful way possible, thus truly emulating the principle taught in the laws of *cheilev*.

The Rebbe writes:
Sefer HaSichot 5750, pp. 481-482

The preparations for Shabbat (which we must enjoy with delightful food and drink) are done by the women (and also by the daughters who help their mothers), to the extent that during the whole week, starting from the beginning of the week, women think about and plan how to prepare for Shabbat in the nicest and most beautiful way. This accords with *Beit Shammai*,[124] who "explained that one should remember Shabbat from the first day of the week, so that if one comes upon a nice item, one should set it aside for Shabbat."

Note that this conduct, according to *Beit Shammai*, is a glorification of the observance of the commandment that is done more by women than men, who conduct themselves according to *Beit Hillel*.[124] As we find, there are several *mitzvot*

---

124 [*Beit Shammai* was one of the major schools of thought in the Talmud; *Beit Hillel* was another major school of thought, whose opinion was usually the opposite of that of *Beit Shammai*.]

that women observe more meticulously, and whose observance they glorify, more than men do. It is possible to say that one of the reasons for this is that since they realize that there are several *mitzvot* that only men are obligated to perform (all positive *mitzvot* that must be performed during a particular time period), they put more effort than men do into glorifying their observance of those *mitzvot* that they – as well as men — are commanded to do.

* * *

In connection with increasing in matters of holiness, in giving charity and studying Torah:

Concerning charity — they give prepared food to poor people and to their household from the food and drink that is in their home. In addition, it is known that the attributes of compassion and kindness (two of the three signs of this nation, "bashful, compassionate, and kind") are part of women's nature more than they are part of men's. Therefore, they put more effort into doing the commandment of charity, both in encouraging their husbands to increase their observance of the commandment of charity, and in giving charity from the money that they earn themselves (as is the custom nowadays in several homes, where the women assist in earning a livelihood, so that they will be able to increase even more in charity and in hospitality to guests).

In particular, as has been mentioned recently, it is worthwhile and proper to affix a charity box to the kitchen, where the woman prepares food for the whole family, in order to serve as a reminder to observe the commandment of charity, through which God's blessing in matters of livelihood is increased, as it is stated, "Give the tithe (*aser*) so that you will become rich (*shetit'asher*)."

Concerning studying Torah, as the *Gemara* states,[125] "What is the merit of women? They bring their sons to the

---

125 *Berachot* 17a, *Sotah* 21a

synagogue and their husbands to the place of study and wait for their husbands until they return from the place of study." Women encourage and motivate their sons and also their husbands — in their special way of heartfelt warmth – to further increase in establishing times for studying Torah, even if it diminishes the amount of time that they devote to earning a livelihood. Through this, God's blessings throughout the home are increased that much more.

STUDY QUESTIONS:

1. How do women prepare for Shabbat in an especially beautiful way?

2. What is a possible reason for this especially beautiful manner of preparation for Shabbat?

3. What are two other *mitzvot* that women observe in an especially beautiful manner?

4. Which of the three attributes that are characteristic of the Jewish nation are part of women's nature more than they are part of men's?

5. What practice does the Rebbe suggest as a reminder to observe the commandment of charity?

6. What special roles do women play in encouraging their husbands and sons to study Torah?

Parashat Tzav

THE HOLY TEMPLE SERVICE
BENEFITS THE ENTIRE JEWISH NATION

Parashat Tzav presents a continuation of the laws presented in the previous Torah portion. These laws describe the procedures that the *kohanim* must follow in bringing the ritual sacrifices.

In the following letter, the Rebbe explains the parallel between the rituals that were carried out in the *Mishkan* and the conduct of a Jewish home. Although the *kohanim* performed the rituals within the confines of the *Mishkan*, the holiness generated by their work permeated the surroundings and benefited the entire Jewish nation. Similarly, every Jew has an obligation to bring holiness to his/her surroundings. This process begins with making one's own home a Godly place – a job that is done mainly by the woman, the *akeret habayit*. By bringing holiness into the conduct of her home, she brings God's blessings into the home and hastens the time when the Holy Temple will be rebuilt and the *kohanim* will once again perform their service.

The Rebbe writes:
Likkutei Sichot vol. 2, pp. 683-684

The Book of *Vayikra* is called *Torat Kohanim* (the laws pertaining to *kohanim*) and the Book of Sacrifices. The idea behind this is:

Jews in general, and every Jew in particular, must be like a *kohen*, as God has instructed,[126] "You shall be to Me a

---

126 [Exodus 19:6]

kingdom of <u>kohanim</u>." Just as a *kohen* has been purified in order to devote himself to the holy service, not only for himself but also for his brethren — the entire Jewish nation — so too, every Jew has been purified to serve God and also has a responsibility to those around him.

<u>The service of God</u> does not mean to dissociate oneself and exclude oneself from the world. It means to serve God <u>in</u> the world and <u>using</u> the world — beginning with one's own home, which is conducted in such a way that God's Presence dwells there — as the Torah says,[127] "They shall make a Sanctuary for Me so that I may dwell among them."

This is achieved through conduct that is analogous to <u>ritual sacrifices</u>.

The idea of ritual sacrifices was as follows: One took items from his belongings — a sheep, flour, olive oil, wine, salt, etc. — and made a ritual sacrifice from them: a *korban-olah* (burnt offering) that is totally for God, as well as a *korban-shelamim* (peace offering) of which part is offered on the altar, and the rest, the *kohen* and the person who brought the ritual sacrifice eat in a state of ritual purity.

A Jewish home, in all its details, must be conducted in such a manner, and if it is, then God's Presence dwells there, and the home is blessed materially and spiritually.

Accomplishing this in life depends mainly on, and is the primary task of, the Jewish woman, the *akeret habayit*: to bring God's presence into the home and into family life, and to bring up the children in that spirit.

May God help you carry out your task to the full extent with Chassidic warmth and liveliness.

By doing so, one hastens the time when the *Beit Hamikdash* will be rebuilt, and the holy service will again be performed,

---

127 [Exodus 25:8]

when the true and complete redemption will come through our righteous *Mashiach*, speedily in our days.

STUDY QUESTIONS:

1. What is the unique role of a *kohen*, and how can every Jew emulate it?

2. Is the main approach to serving God to isolate oneself from the world or to be involved with and improve the world?

3. What aspects of the ritual sacrifices are relevant to our service of God today?

4. What are the benefits of serving God in a manner analogous to bringing ritual sacrifices?

5. What can the Jewish woman do to bring God's presence into her home?

Parashat Shemini

THE VITAL IMPORTANCE
OF THE OBSERVANCE OF *KASHRUT*

Parashat Shemini discusses at length the laws of *kashrut*, i.e., which foods are permissible and prohibited for Jews to eat. The Torah portion gives rules for determining which species of animals and fish may and may not be eaten. It also gives a long list of species of non-kosher birds.

In the discourse from which the following section is taken, the Rebbe explains that laxity in the observance of *kashrut* leads to a descent in spiritual level from one generation to the next. This is because the food a person eats affects much more than his/her physical well-being; it also affects character traits and attitudes. Therefore, if one eats non-kosher food, one will not have the spiritual strength that is required to overcome any negative character traits and attitudes that he/she may have. Accordingly, when an entire generation is not careful in its observance of *kashrut*, the people of that generation accrue negative spiritual qualities. They will then transmit these qualities to the following generation, and if that next generation is also not careful about *kashrut*, they will accrue additional negative spiritual qualities. In this way, a laxity in observance of *kashrut* leads to a chain-like descent in the spiritual levels of the generations.

The Rebbe describes how the level of observance of this commandment is almost entirely determined by the women, since they are usually the most involved with food preparation. Jewish women, therefore, have the vitally important responsibility, as well as the capability, of safeguarding the observance of *kashrut*. Their careful observance of this law and their positive influence on their family in this matter benefit the entire Jewish nation.

The Rebbe writes:
Likkutei Sichot vol. 13, pp. 260-262

The second explanation[128] for the deterioration in the spiritual situation is also connected with a matter that lies almost entirely in the hands of Jewish women.

It is explained in Torah books and also books of natural science that the character and attributes of a person are affected in large measure by the type of foods and drinks that he consumes. That is because the food becomes transformed into his own flesh and blood. Just as the foods one selects to eat affect his physical health, they also affect his spiritual character. As our Sages have written, through eating the meat of an animal of prey, the character of cruelty is transferred to the person's soul.

Just as the foods one eats affect one's character and attributes, similarly, the foods also affect one's mind — the manner in which one grasps and understands concepts. If he feeds himself coarse and contaminated food, it evokes coarseness and dullness in his mind. In contrast, his mind is clearer and he understands in a more refined manner when he eats refined foods, as is explained in Torah books and also in books on natural science. Therefore, it is understood that non-kosher foods, foods forbidden by the Torah, have a maximally damaging influence on the refinement and purity of the Jewish mind. This kind of food can even cause influences and inclinations in the mind that are contrary to Torah.

This makes it easier to understand the reason for the descent in the generations. The first issue (not properly

---

128 [The first explanation for the deterioration in the spiritual situation is presented in the chapter on *Parashat Metzora*, page 151.]

observing the laws of family purity, God forbid) results in the deficiency of an anti-Torah and anti-Jewish manner which affect the "spiritual garments" in which the child is born. After that, the soul still has freedom of choice and therefore it has the capability, with an expenditure of energy and the proper effort, to overcome the inborn, anti-Torah nature of the "garments." The soul can do this if only it would act with strength, and the soul *has* the strength!

Why indeed do we not see in all Jews this overpowering of the soul over the nature of the "garments?"

The answer is connected with the second issue. During his life after he is born, he does not observe the laws of *kashrut*, and through eating non-kosher foods that the Torah forbids, he acquires non-kosher spiritual qualities. Therefore, it is understandable why these spiritual qualities will not allow and leave no possibility for him to exercise the above-mentioned power of his soul.

Even those who were born in purity and holiness — if they utilize their free choice to, God forbid, eat non-kosher food that the Torah forbids, then they corrupt, God forbid, the pure "garments" of their souls with their anti-Torah ways, and so on.

The observance of *kashrut* in food and drink depends mainly on the *akeret habayit*. In general, the conduct of the world is that it is the woman who is involved with preparation of food, with matters of the kitchen, and so on.

When the Jewish woman reveals within herself and evokes the strong will and resolution that all foods and drinks in the home must be kosher in accordance with God's commandments, then she will be able to carry out this resolution with the fullest measure of success.

Furthermore, she will be able to carry it out not only within her home. It is possible that her husband, or someone else in the family, is meanwhile not in a condition to comprehend the vital necessity of the observance of *kashrut*. Nevertheless, if she establishes and asserts that in the kitchen and in the entire house, the laws of *kashrut* of food and drink will be fully observed, this will induce a change in the spiritual character, and will have an effect on the thought process of the husband (or on another member of the household), to the extent that he will observe the laws of *kashrut* outside the home as well.

In particular, she should endeavor to influence him in this direction with persuasive speech.

The first issue that was mentioned as a factor in the descent in the spiritual level from one generation to the next — observance of the laws of family purity — is a matter which concerns the individual, as well as the entire household, the building of the Jewish home, and therefore also the entire Jewish nation (which is based on the Jewish home). Similarly, the second issue — observance of the laws of *kashrut* of food and drink — is a fundamental issue that affects the individual, the family, and the entire Jewish nation.

STUDY QUESTIONS:

1.   What effect does the food a person eats have on her body, physically and spiritually?

2.   What effects could eating non-kosher foods have on a person?

3.   How could the negative effect of a person's eating non-kosher food affect her children?

4.   How could the negative effect of a person's eating non-kosher food influence one's observance of other *mitzvot*?

5.	What is the most effective approach for the *akeret habayit* to use to help her family observe *kaashrut* better?

6.	How could someone's observance of *kashrut* only at home affect his observance of the rest of the *mitzvot*?

7.	What are some far-reaching consequences of one person's observance of *kashrut*?

Parashat Tazria

THE POWER OF SHABBAT CANDLES
TO OVERCOME IMPURITY

Parashat Tazria describes in detail the laws of *tzara'at*. *Tzara'at* is an illness that existed in the times of the *Beit Hamikdash*. It had physical symptoms – various types of skin lesions – but its origin was spiritual. Caused by certain sins, the cure was the patient's repentance. While the patient had this illness, he was ritually impure. One of the laws of this impurity is that if he goes into a house, all the items in the house become ritually impure. The Mishna (cited in the discourse referred to below) tells us that he could transmit his impurity to the items in the house only if he was in the house for the amount of time it takes to light Shabbat candles. Thus, there is some connection between lighting Shabbat candles and the transmission of the impurity of *tzara'at*.

In the discourse whose concluding section is presented below, the Rebbe explains that the Shabbat candles have a spiritual quality that prevents the acquisition of the impurity of *tzara'at*. To explain how this can be, the Rebbe discusses the inner spiritual significance of the Shabbat candles as well as that of *tzara'at*. In view of the tremendous spiritual power of the Shabbat candles, the Rebbe issues a call that every Jewish woman and girl – from the age at which she can first understand the meaning of Shabbat – should light candles every Shabbat. The light of these Shabbat candles will dispel the darkness of exile and bring the redemption.

The Rebbe writes:
Likkutei Sichot vol. 17, pp. 145-147

This is the special quality of the Shabbat candles, which have the characteristic of "Making peace in the world"[129] with more intensity. The idea of peace in the world, perceiving that the true reality of the world is Godliness, is accomplished through the Shabbat candles more than it is through other *mitzvot*. As it says in the *Zohar*,[130] "A commandment is a candle. What is the commandment-candle? That...is the Shabbat candle." The Shabbat candles have the characteristic of "a commandment is a candle" — lighting up the world — with more intensity than other *mitzvot* do, even those that are connected with a physical candle.

It is possible to say that this is the deeper reason for the fact that, in connection with the peace in the home, which the light of Shabbat candles brings about, the words[131] "so that one will not stumble on wood or stone" are used. Why are the particular words 'wood' and 'stone' used? These words hint at the verse,[132] "They say to the wood, 'You are my father,' and to the stone, 'You have borne us,' " i.e., from the wood or stone, an idol is made, God forbid. This is the accomplishment of the Shabbat candles — "that one will not stumble on wood or stone." The existence of the wood or stone themselves (before they are illuminated by the Shabbat candles) may make someone stumble, God forbid, into thinking that they (the wood or stone) God forbid exist on their own, and have their own power, to the extent that one calls the wood, "my father" and says to the stone, "You have borne us" (an actual idol, God forbid).

---

129 [Earlier in this discourse, the Rebbe cites the statement, "The whole Torah was given in order to make peace in the world" (Maimonides, *Mishna Torah*, Laws of Chanukah, Chapter 4, paragraph 14).]

130 Vol. 2, p.166a

131 The *Shulchan Aruch*[*HaRav* (Chapter 263, paragraph 1) states that the Shabbat candles illuminate the home so that one will not stumble on wood or on stone.]

132 Jeremiah 2:27, [*Artscroll Tanach*, Mesorah Publications, Ltd., Brooklyn, New York, 2003]

The light of the Shabbat candles, whose "commandment-candle" and effect of creating "peace in the world" affect the physicality of the world in a revealed way, ensures "that one will not stumble on wood or stone." That is because they allow us to perceive that the wood and stone, like everything in the world, are controlled by the Master of the world and must be used for matters of holiness.

According to the above, the special connection between the purification from the impurity of *tzara'at* and the Shabbat candles can also be understood.

The impurity of *tzara'at* is one of the most severe forms of impurity, and therefore, one of the laws concerning one who has *tzara'at* is that, "He shall sit alone, outside of the camp where he lives." He is sent out of all three camps [in which the Jews dwelled], and in that location, "he must sit <u>alone</u>," such that other impure people should not sit with him. The place for one with *tzara'at* is even outside of the camp of <u>other impure people</u>, that is, he is completely excluded from the camp of holiness.

The reason for this is that the sin which causes *tzara'at* — slanderous speech — is very severe since it causes, in the words of Maimonides, "speaking against God and denying fundamental principles of faith." Through that one is, God forbid, completely torn away from God.

Therefore, it is specifically the Shabbat candles that prevent the spread of this type of impurity, because they have a strong effect on the physicality of the world. The effect of the candles is so strong that they, in particular, ensure "that one will not stumble on wood or on stone" — which represents idol worship, God forbid (as described earlier at length) — and therefore they preclude the impurity of *tzara'at*, which is connected with "speaking against God and denying fundamental principles of Judaism."

The explanation that [the Rebbe's] father gave in his commentary, that the idea of lighting Shabbat candles is analogous to <u>purification</u> by a *kohen* of one who has *tzara'at*, is applicable to our topic. Not only do the Shabbat candles have the power to <u>prevent</u> the spread of the impurity of *tzara'at*, but even more — they also have the power to make the utensils in the house remain pure from the impurity of *tzara'at*.

According to the example of purification by a *kohen*, this represents the transformation of darkness into light — "His sins are transformed into merits." The condition of "He shall sit alone..." which illustrates the ultimate descent, as mentioned earlier, becomes "He shall dwell alone" in a positive sense – "It is a nation that will dwell <u>in solitude</u>..."[133] "[Thus Israel shall dwell] secure, <u>solitary</u>, in the likeness of Jacob..."[134] which is the ultimate blessing.

Similarly, with regard to the darkness of the exile, specifically the doubled and redoubled darkness of the generation that is at the heels of the *Mashiach* — through the light of the Shabbat candles, we will light up the darkness of the exile and nullify it. Moreover, we will attain the redemption and the building of the *Beit Hamikdash*, and the prophecies of "God will show you the candles of Zion,"[135] and "God will be an eternal light for you"[136] will be fulfilled, to the extent that the darkness of the exile itself will be transformed to light — "night shines like the day."[137]

From all that has been mentioned, it is understood that in the present time, when the darkness of the exile is so great and thick, it is especially important that <u>every</u> Jewish daughter (including those in those circles where the daughters have been accustomed until now to begin lighting

---

133 Numbers 23:9. [This verse is part of Bil'am's blessing of the Jewish nation.]
134 [Deuteronomy 33:28. This verse is part of Moses ' blessing of the Jewish nation.]
135 *Yalkut Shimoni*, beginning of *Parashat Beha'alotecha*
136 Isaiah 60:19
137 Psalms 139:12

candles only after their wedding, and until then, they would fulfill their obligation through their mother's candle-lighting), should light candles herself as soon as she is old enough that we can explain to her the meaning of the Shabbat and *Yom Tov* candles.

[At this point, the Rebbe inserted the following footnote in bold text:] **It should be pointed out, and this is of fundamental importance: In a home in which, for whatever reason, the mother does not light candles, <u>according to all opinions</u> the daughter must light (at least, once she has reached the age of Bat Mitzvah), and therefore, there should be as great an effort as possible in this matter. If the daughters in Torah-observant homes in her surroundings do not light candles, it is understood that success in this effort will be most difficult to achieve, as can be seen in practical reality. <u>And these words should be sufficient for an understanding person.</u>**

The light of the Shabbat candles, along with the blessing that she will make on them, will illuminate her life, so that she will realize and remember, as she says in the blessing, that God is the "King of the world." This increases the certainty that when she is ready to get married, "God will be an <u>eternal</u> light for you," she will — as the *akeret habayit* — build and establish her home according to God's will, upon the foundations of Torah and its commandments.

An additional reason for the necessity that *all* Jewish girls light candles:

As mentioned earlier,[138] through lighting candles, one merits children (and sons-in-law) who are Torah scholars. Therefore, in former times, when the practice was that the parents made the decision regarding a marriage partner for their daughter, the most important factor was the merit of the

---

138 [In another part of the discourse not excerpted here]

mother's Shabbat candles, so that her daughter would marry a Torah scholar.

In the present time, when for a variety of reasons, the practical reality is that — whether or not we would like it to be so — regarding a marriage partner, the daughter decides mainly on her own, it is even more vital that she herself should light candles, and the "commandment-candle" that she lights will give her the merit that she should marry a Torah scholar.

In the present time, when even in Torah-observant homes it is not always a certainty that the parents' opinion will have a decisive influence on their daughter when she gets older, we must strive and endeavor to the maximum extent that as early as possible, i.e., as soon as she reaches the age at which she can be trained in lighting the Shabbat candles, she light candles on the eve of every Shabbat and *Yom Tov*.

This also strengthens the Torah's assurance that she will be raised "for Torah, for the marriage canopy, and for good deeds" and that she will marry a Torah scholar.

STUDY QUESTIONS:

1.   What is the connection between Shabbat candles and making peace in the world?

2.   What potential pitfall would one encounter in the absence of the illumination of the Shabbat candles?

3.   What fundamental concept do the Shabbat candles enable us to grasp?

4.   Since the impurity of *tzara'at* is so severe, what must a person afflicted with it do, which other impure people do not need to do?

5.   What is the very severe sin that caused a person to get *tzara'at*?

6.   What aspect of Shabbat candles refutes the erroneous concept that brings about *tzara'at*?

7.   What effect do the Shabbat candles have on the spiritual darkness of the world?

8.   Why is it so important that young girls light Shabbat candles (two main reasons)?

Parashat Metzora

THE VITAL IMPORTANCE OF THE OBSERVANCE
OF THE LAWS OF FAMILY PURITY

Parashat Metzora discusses how various bodily discharges can render a person spiritually impure. Some of the laws in this category deal with the spiritual impurity that a woman acquires if she has a discharge of blood, as well as the procedure for purification from this type of impurity. These laws form the basis of the laws of family purity. The laws of family purity govern the nature of the relationship between a husband and wife, and their observance affects the spiritual and physical characteristics of their children.

In the discourse from which the following section is taken, the Rebbe explains how laxity in the observance of the laws of family purity has led to a descent in the spiritual level of recent generations. In particular, laxity in a couple's observance of these laws leads to spiritual deficiencies in their children. As a result, such children have a more difficult time resisting the efforts of the evil inclination. They are vulnerable to the influence of immoral ideas.

The Rebbe describes how in practical reality, the level of observance of this commandment is almost entirely determined by the woman. Moreover, if a woman truly desires to observe these laws, she will be able to ensure their observance. Thus, Jewish women have a vitally important role in promoting the spiritual well-being of the Jewish people. This role and influence extends not only to the current generation, but also to future generations.

The Rebbe writes:
Likkutei Sichot vol. 13, pp. 258-260

The question is asked in Torah books, and is asked even more by people, about the condition of Judaism and the observance of Torah and its commandments in recent generations: How did it come to be that such a low level prevails in our own Jewish circles, such a spiritual lowliness as is described in the end of Tractate *Sotah*?

Two explanations[139] are given for this.

One explanation is that in order for Jewish souls to have the character that they should have in this world, such that it will be more difficult for the evil inclination to do its harmful work, Jewish children must be born in purity and holiness. However, if there is a deficiency in the necessary observance of the laws and details of family purity, then there is a negative effect on the souls that are born afterward — there is a deficiency in the refinement and purity of the spiritual garments through which the soul exerts its effects and expresses itself.

From this comes the phenomenon of such strange ideas as, for example, the claim that there can be a "conversion" — the birth of a new Jew,[140] even when it is done "not in accordance with Jewish law," which is contrary to simple human understanding. Another example is the statement that the existence of Jews is not connected with study of Torah and observance of its commandments, even though it is clear that it is on this that the existence and life of Jews depend, just like fish in the sea, whose whole life depends on water, and they can absolutely not exist without it, and so on.

---

139 [The first explanation is given in the excerpt presented here. The second explanation is given in the excerpt presented in connection with *Parashat Shemini, page 137.*]

140 In the words of our Sages, "A convert who has converted is comparable to a newborn baby" (*Yevamot* 22a [and other sources]).

The practical observance of the laws of family purity lies naturally in the hands of Jewish women; from the man it requires that he facilitate the observance and make it easy, and he should certainly agree to it; he should not oppose it, God forbid. Moreover, if the woman truly wants and consents to it, she can certainly implement it. The peace in the home is solidified and strengthened through this. In particular, the laws and details of family purity, with extensive explanations of its tremendous urgency and importance, are published in brochures in many languages and are accessible to everyone.

This is the great mission and duty that Jewish women have — to make an effort that Jewish daughters observe the laws of family purity. For besides the fact that this commandment is a foundation — a foundation of holiness in family life — it affects as well the health of the soul (and health of the body) and the purity of the Jewish children's souls — it affects and is drawn through all Jewish generations, through Jewish eternity. Children will be born, who will grow up and build their own Jewish homes — "an eternal edifice," grandchildren, and so on.

STUDY QUESTIONS:

1. What effect does deficiency in observance of the laws of family purity have on the souls of Jewish children?

2. What are some strange ideas that could be thought of by someone whose soul has been negatively affected?

3. What analogy shows how vital it is for a Jew to observe the commandments of the Torah?

4. Which person in the family has the main responsibility to ensure that the laws of family purity are properly observed?

5.   What benefits to family life come from proper observance of the laws of family purity?

6.   How has a deficiency in observance of the laws of family purity led to a descent in the spiritual level from one generation to the next?

7.   What are the far reaching positive effects of proper observance of the laws of family purity?

Parashat Acharei Mot

SYNTHESIS OF THE SPIRITUAL
AND THE PHYSICAL

The first words of *Parashat Acharei Mot* refer to the death of two of the sons of Aaron when they entered the Holy of Holies of the *Mishkan* in an improper way. The commentaries offer various opinions of what was done improperly. In the discourse from which the following excerpt is taken, the Rebbe explains that all of these opinions have one common underlying theme: the sons of Aaron entered the Holy of Holies with the sole intention of satisfying their own desire for spiritual elevation and closeness to God. They entered this most holy place without regard for God's desire that Jews should serve Him from within the world, elevating its physical nature by observing His commandments.

The proper way, therefore, to enter the Holy of Holies is to go with the intention of fulfilling God's will, rather than satisfying one's own spiritual desires. The procedure the *Kohen Gadol* followed in his service on Yom Kippur, part of which is described in this Torah portion, illustrates the correct approach. When the *Kohen Gadol* left the Holy of Holies, he said a short prayer on behalf of the Jewish people, asking God to fulfill their material needs. Thus, the *Kohen Gadol's* entrance into this most holy place – a sublime spiritual experience – was inextricably connected with a prayer for the Jews' material needs.

In the following excerpt, the Rebbe explains a practical lesson that we can derive from these ideas. There is certainly no contradiction between increasing our spiritual connection to God and having our material needs fulfilled. On the contrary, we must realize that the fulfillment of our material needs depends on the quality of our spiritual connection to God. It is the woman's duty to explain to her family that it is specifically through increasing in the observance of God's commandments that they merit having their material needs fulfilled generously.

The Rebbe writes:
Likkutei Sichot vol. 3, pp. 992-993

The lesson that is derived from the connection between the *Kohen Gadol*'s entrance into the Holy of Holies with his exit from there relates not only to the service involving material matters [i.e., the prayer that the *Kohen Gadol* said when he exited from there] — it also relates to the fact that the material matters in a Jew's life are <u>themselves</u> connected with the entrance into the Most Inner Place.[141] This connection between the spiritual and material matters in a Jew's life is due to the fact that a Jew receives everything that he has — even the aspects of material sustenance such as children, health, and income — directly from God. As the verse[142] states, "If you will follow My decrees and observe My commandments...then <u>I will provide</u> your rains in their time..." A Jew can receive the rains in their time, etc., only through the observance of Torah and its commandments.

The calculation that "Peace will be with me, though I walk as my heart sees fit,"[143] i.e., that he will receive his material sustenance even when he follows the desires of his heart, rather than the requirements of holiness — this calculation can be valid only temporarily, because ultimately, the vitality of a Jew must have a direct connection with Godliness.

This connection between spiritual and material matters is hinted at in the connection between "entrance into the Most

---

141 [In Hebrew, *lifnai v'lifnim,* a phrase that refers to the Holy of Holies.]
142 [Leviticus 26:3, *Artscroll Tanach,* Mesorah Publications, Ltd., Brooklyn, New York, 2003]
143 [Deuteronomy 29:18]

Inner Place" and "when he emerges from the Holy of Holies." It is only after the *Kohen Gadol* was in the Most Inner Place, and through his being there, that he could pray for and request material livelihood when he came out. Furthermore, the livelihood that is received is in abundance, without limitations, because it comes from the Most Inner Place.

As mentioned [earlier in this discourse], the *Kohen Gadol* must be married in order to be allowed to enter the Holy of Holies. There is deep meaning in this. The proper entrance into the Holy of Holies and the consequent "emerging in peace," which is the purpose of the entrance, depends on the influence of the Jewish women. It is the privilege and duty of Jewish women and daughters to influence their husbands and children to make their entrance into the Holy of Holies [i.e. the very spiritual environment] connected with their exit from there [into the worldly environment].

In particular, a Jewish woman must not worry that if her husband prays an hour or more longer, or if he learns Torah an hour or more longer, there might be a deficiency in material matters. Similarly, there is no place for the worry that if one educates the children such that they learn Torah the whole day, they might have difficulty supporting themselves, and so on. On the contrary, they must explain to their husbands and children that it is specifically through increasing in the observance of Torah and its commandments, [as expressed] in the [verse][144] "If you will follow My decrees and observe My commandments," that the "I will provide your rains in their time..." will come.

STUDY QUESTIONS:

1. What is the direct origin of a Jew's material sustenance?

---

144 [Numbers 26:3-4]

2.   What must a Jew do in order to receive blessings in material sustenance?

3.   What erroneous belief might one have in connection with his receipt of material sustenance?

4.   What action that the Kohen Gadol performed enabled him to pray for material sustenance afterward?

5.   What is the significance of the fact that the Kohen Gadol must be married in order to perform the service in the Holy of Holies?

6.   What influence should a wife have on her husband to facilitate the family's receipt of material sustenance?

Parashat Kedoshim

In *Parashat Kedoshim*, a key commandment in the Torah is stated: "You shall love your fellow as yourself."[145] Rabbi Akiva said that this is a basic principle of the Torah. Hillel, the great rabbi of the Mishna, also explained the fundamental importance of this commandment, as illustrated by the following story:[146] Once a non-Jew, who was considering converting, came to Hillel and asked that he teach him the whole Torah while standing on one foot. Hillel answered him, "What is hateful to you, do not do to your friend. This is the entire Torah, and the rest is commentary." Hillel's answer is an alternative way of expressing the idea of love for one's fellow Jew.

In the following excerpt, the Rebbe gives a practical suggestion for women on how to fulfill this commandment of loving one's fellow Jew. The Rebbe also describes the blessings that God will bestow upon the woman who helps her fellow Jew.

The Rebbe writes:
Likkutei Sichot, vol. 4, pp. 1279-1280

The woman must realize that in order to have success in conducting the affairs of the home, she should set aside for herself some time every day, at least a few minutes, to take an interest in and help her friends in matters of Judaism and also

---

145 Leviticus 19:18, *Artscroll Tanach,* Mesorah Publications, Ltd., Brooklyn, New York, 2003
146 *Shabbat* 31a

in material matters. Concern with the material matters of another person is a spiritual matter for oneself.

The reward for her doing a favor for another Jew, man or woman, is very great because of God's great love for every Jew. About each Jew it is stated,[147] " 'I loved you,' said God," and the Baal Shem Tov explains that this love is of the type that parents feel for their only son. Therefore, as a reward for her helping another Jew, God will reward her many times over, so that all the dealings of her home will be successful, and she will raise her children, together with her husband, to Torah, to marriage, and good deeds.

STUDY QUESTIONS:

1. What activity should a woman do daily to help other Jewish women?

2. What benefit will accrue to her if she does perform this activity?

3. What is the difference between the status of one's own material needs and the status of another person's material needs?

4. How is the relationship of God to every Jew similar to the relationship of parents to their only child?

5. Why is God's reward for helping another Jew so generous?

---

147 *Malachi* 1:2

Parashat Emor

HOW WOMEN SHOULD RELATE
TO THE OUTSIDE WORLD

Parashat Emor tells the story of the son of Shlomit bat Divri. This son cursed God, using God's holiest name. As punishment God commanded that he be executed.

Why was this son so angry that he made such a severe curse? *Rashi* explains that the son's mother was from the tribe of Dan, but his father was an Egyptian – a non-Jew. The son tried to set up his tent in the territory of the tribe of Dan. However, the people of Dan did not allow him, because he would be considered a member of the tribe of Dan only if his <u>father</u> was from that tribe. He brought the case to Moses' court, which confirmed this ruling. As a result the son was very angry.

Rashi further explains what led to this unfortunate situation in which a Jewish woman had a child with a non-Jewish man. *Rashi* explains that this woman's name hints at her character. The name Shlomit is related to the Hebrew word for hello; she used to say hello and greet everyone. The name Divri is related to the Hebrew word for speaking; she used to talk a lot, and speak with everybody. Because of her inappropriate and excessive sociability, she became involved in this improper situation.

This story shows that a woman should not act excessively social, at least in public. On the other hand, a woman would not want to be completely confined to her home. What is the proper balance between these two extremes?

In the following discourse, the Rebbe addresses this question. He quotes a prophecy that says in the future, old men and women will sit in the streets of Jerusalem. One may wonder: why would the women be out in the street, when ideally – it would seem – they should stay modestly within their homes? We see, however, that women do need to leave their homes. As children, they receive their education at Jewish girls' schools, something firmly established by leaders of recent generations. As adults, their going out has also become necessary in the areas of Jewish education and helping others strengthen their observance of Torah.

When women are involved in these activities, they must be careful to act modestly. Also, they should be guided by the words of the above-mentioned prophecy, which speaks of the city of Jerusalem. The name Jerusalem (*Yerushalayim*) is related to the words for perfect fear (*yirah shleimah*); thus, women should act with wholehearted fear of Heaven. With such an approach, they will succeed in their activities, and help bring the *Mashiach*.

The Rebbe writes:
Likkutei Sichot vol. 21, pp. 379-380

The Gemara says that when Rabban Gamliel, Rabbi Elazar ben Azariah, Rabbi Yehoshua, and Rabbi Akiva arrived at the Temple Mount, the site of the ruined Holy Temple, they saw a fox coming out of the location of the Holy of Holies — the holiest part of the Holy Temple. The first three rabbis began to cry but Rabbi Akiva beamed with joy. They asked him why he was so joyous. He replied, "In the prophecy of Uriah it is written that, 'Zion shall be ploughed like a field[148],' and in the book of Zechariah it is written, 'Old men and old women will yet sit in the streets of Jerusalem[149].' Until the prophecy of Uriah was fulfilled, I was afraid that the prophecy of Zechariah might not be fulfilled. Now that the prophecy of Uriah has been fulfilled, it is a certainty that the prophecy of

148 [Jeremiah 26:18]
149 [Zecharia 8:4]

Zechariah will be fulfilled" — in the future redemption, may it happen speedily in our days, amen.

The question arises: The prophet Zechariah tells us that Jerusalem will yet be built upon its former site, and old men will sit in the streets of Jerusalem; but what does it mean that also <u>women</u> will sit in the streets of Jerusalem? This seems to be the opposite of, "The honor of a king's daughter is internal,"[150] i.e., the honor of a Jewish woman is to be found privately, within her home, and not on the street.

We can similarly ask about the prophecy of the prophet Jeremiah regarding the future redemption, "There will yet be heard in the cities of Judea and in the streets of Jerusalem...the voice of the groom and the voice of the bride.[151]" The voice of a woman in the streets seems to be the opposite of modesty.

We can understand this according to the explanation of *Tosafot* that the prophecy of "Old men and old women will yet sit..." was said regarding the period after the resurrection of the dead, and in that time, "Also his enemies will make peace with him." That is, the evil inclination will also make peace with the Jew's desire to serve God. Therefore, the precaution that currently applies — "the honor of a king's daughter is internal" — will be unnecessary at that time, and then the prophecies, "Old men and old women will yet sit in the streets of Jerusalem" and "There will yet be heard...the voice of the groom and the voice of the bride" will be able to be fulfilled.

All of this was said regarding the future. However, everything that we learn in Torah has a specific lesson for <u>us</u>; every idea in Torah can and must provide a lesson in <u>our</u> lives as well.

There are those who ask, "Why do we devote ourselves so much to the education of girls these days — and to such an

---

150 [Psalms 45:14]
151 [Jeremiah 33:10-11]

extent that we have not seen in the previous generations — being that this requires that the Jewish daughter must, to a certain measure, go out of the 'inwardness' in order to receive this education in a school for girls?"

Moreover, Jewish women today are employed in work for the good of the community, for Torah and Judaism, and they must often go out of the four cubits of their "her honor is internal" territory in order to successfully carry out this work.

Nevertheless, we see that this was carried out in the previous generation according to the instructions of the true leaders of the generation. It was based on their instructions that schools for girls were established in a similar manner to schools for Jewish boys (with a different curriculum), although such education for girls is connected with their going out of the home to school.

However, when a situation arises of "It is time to act for God,"[152] a time of necessity for Judaism, and of sanctifying God's name — in such a "time to act for God," the Torah leaders utilize special means to carry this out. The leaders of the generation saw and felt the urgent need to establish schools for Jewish daughters, in order to give them the religious Jewish Torah education that the home by itself is not able to sufficiently provide, and in this way, to bring up future religious Jewish generations.

The activities of women in working for Judaism and Torah education are also things that were encouraged and strengthened by the leaders of the generation; the same is true regarding the organization of women's groups — in a way of modesty and devotedness. Just as the merit of the accomplishments of the Jewish women in those days brought about the release of the Jews from Egypt, similarly their good deeds will also now help bring the complete redemption.

---

152 [Psalms 119:126]

The reward for performing a commandment is similar to the commandment itself that one performs. In order to receive the promised reward of "old men and old women will sit in the streets of Jerusalem" (a reward that includes women as well as men), the service and observance of the commandments must be done in a way that is similar to this reward.

Today, this is the task and duty of Jewish women: they give up their time and effort to carry out the important Jewish duties — in a modest way — through the "streets of Jerusalem," through a "Jerusalem" that everyone can and must build for himself. That is, the work should be performed with "complete fear" (*Yerushalayim*), with the completeness of fear of God. Together with this, the work should be carried out "with breadth" (*rechovot*[153]) — and through that, one will succeed, and also prepare the path for our righteous *Mashiach*.

STUDY QUESTIONS:

1. Why was Rabbi Akiva happy when he saw a fox coming out of the location of the destroyed Holy of Holies?

2. What is puzzling about the prophecy that old women will sit in the streets of Jerusalem?

3. What aspect of the period after the resurrection of the dead makes precautions of modesty less necessary?

4. On what basis were schools for Jewish girls established?

---

153 [The word *rechovot* means 'streets,' but it shares its root with the word *rachav*, which means 'wide.']

5.   In what manner should women of today conduct their activities in working outside the home for Judaism and Torah education?

6.   What is the reward for Jewish women's performing their work outside the home with complete fear of God?

Parashat Behar

BRINGING HOLINESS
INTO EVERYDAY ACTIVITIES

Parashat Behar explains the laws of *Shmitta*, which apply to farming in the Land of Israel. The Torah tells us that every seventh year is called a *Shmitta* year, in which agricultural work on the Land is prohibited, allowing the Jewish farmers to devote more time to Torah study than they would be able to in an ordinary year.

In the following excerpt from a letter, the Rebbe explains the lesson that we can all derive from this commandment, even if we have no involvement in agricultural work: we should infuse more Godliness into our daily life, thereby transforming even our mundane activities into holy activities. This lesson is particularly applicable in years that are *Shmitta* years, but is relevant at all times. The Rebbe explains the special significance of this commandment for women – that the woman, as the foundation of the home, must increase the holiness in all aspects of home life.

The Rebbe writes:
Likkutei Sichot vol. 7, pp. 358-359

This year is a *Shmitta* year, the seventh year that is sanctified among the years just as the seventh day, Shabbat, is sanctified among the days of the week. However, there is a difference between *Shmitta* and Shabbat — on Shabbat, all types of work (*melachot*[154]) are forbidden, whereas in the *Shmitta* year, one is not allowed to do agricultural work in the

---

154 [The type of work referred to here is any one of the 39 categories of work that the Torah forbids a Jew to perform on Shabbat.]

fields and gardens, but all other types of work in the home and elsewhere are permitted.

The purpose of the *Shmitta* year, as well as the reason for the day of Shabbat, is to set aside a time <u>for God</u> — sanctified for God. That means, first and foremost, that the time that is made available by not doing agricultural work, which was one of the primary occupations of Jews before the time of exile, should be used for matters of Godliness and holiness.

From this follows another important lesson of *Shmitta*. Even in ordinary "weekday" day-to-day life, one should increase in matters of Godliness, to the extent that the entire year can be justifiably described as "for God," similar to Shabbat, which is referred to as "holy for God."

Just as the spirit and holiness of Shabbat must influence all the days of the week, and Shabbat is the source of God's blessings for all the days of the week, similarly, the spirit and holiness of *Shmitta* should be reflected in all the other years. Also, the *Shmitta* year creates channels through which to receive God's blessings even in material necessities.

The meaning of this for the Jewish woman is that although she is not engaged in studying Torah, she can and must increase in all matters of holiness in the home, where she is the *akeret habayit*, as well as in activities that support Torah institutions...

STUDY QUESTIONS:

1.   What is the difference between the kinds of work that may be done on Shabbat, which is the seventh (day) and what may be done during *Shmittah*, which is the seventh (year)?

2.   Since certain types of work may not be done during the *Shmittah* year, how should one spend the time that is made available by not doing that work?

3.   How can the principles of *Shmittah* observance be applied to one's daily life?

4.   How does the *Shmittah* year influence the years that follow it?

5.   What lesson can the Jewish woman derive from the *Shmittah* year in her conduct in the home and in the community?

Parashat Bechukotai

MODEST CONDUCT BRINGS GREAT BLESSINGS

In *Parashat Bechukotai*, God describes the blessings that the Jews will receive if they learn Torah and observe its commandments. At the end of the list of blessings is the main blessing – the greatest of all of them. God says, "I will place My sanctuary among you...I will walk among you, I will be your God and you will be My people."[155]

In the following excerpt from a letter, the Rebbe explains, on the basis of various verses in the Torah, that in order for the above-mentioned blessing to be fulfilled, we must have among ourselves an atmosphere of holiness, purity, and modesty. These qualities are necessary for the Godly presence to rest among the Jews. It is the women who, through their own example, set the tone for modesty in the conduct of the Jewish people. Furthermore, the modest conduct of the mother brings blessings to her children.

The Rebbe writes:
Likkutei Sichot vol. 7, pp. 360-361

Based on the profound statement of the Alter Rebbe, the founder of Chabad Chassidism, that "a Jew must live with the time," i.e., with the time of the weekly Torah portion, the Torah of life, that demonstrates the way ([The word "Torah" is] grammatically related to the word "*hora'ah*," [which means "teaching"]) in daily life, so that every day of the week is enlivened by the Torah portion of that week —

---

155 Leviticus 26:11, 12, *Artscroll Tanach*, Mesorah Publications, Ltd., Brooklyn, New York, 2003

It is worth dwelling on the verses of the Torah portion of this Shabbat, in which the blessings that come as a reward for "you will follow My decrees and observe My commandments" are enumerated. The high point of the blessings is: "I will place My Sanctuary among you...I will walk among you, I will be your God and you will be My people." This blessing is connected with the general observance of Torah and the commandments, according to what is stated in the beginning of the Torah portion, as mentioned above. Nevertheless, the conclusion of the blessings especially underscores the importance of <u>holiness</u>, <u>purity</u>, and <u>modesty</u>, since they are the foundations of the Divine Sanctuary and Divine Presence among the Jews in general, and within every Jew, man and woman, in particular. This is also clearly underscored elsewhere in the Torah: "...so your camp (at home and outside) shall be holy, so that He (God) will not see a shameful thing among you and turn away from behind you."[156]

Our Sages explain clearly that modesty and holiness must be observed in all matters, in speech and even more so in attire and conduct.

It has already been mentioned at various opportunities that Jewish women and daughters set the tone in certain requirements of Jewish life, as we see clearly. This is especially and uniquely so regarding the requirement of modesty, as is mentioned many times in the words of our Sages, to the extent that it is said that the highest satisfaction from children, both materially and spiritually, is connected with the modest conduct of the mother...

STUDY QUESTIONS:

1. What is the connection between a Torah portion and the week in which it is read?

---

156 [Deuteronomy 23:15]

2.   What is the main blessing mentioned in this *parsha*?

3.   The main blessing shows the importance of which particular personal qualities?

4.   What is so important about these qualities?

5.   In which areas of life must one be especially careful to conduct oneself with modesty and holiness?

6.   What is a very great reward for a woman's modest conduct?

.

Parashat Bamidbar

RAISING A GENERATION OF CHILDREN
FOR GOD'S ARMY

In *Parashat Bamidbar*, God commanded Moses to count the Jews. In particular, he was commanded to count men who are twenty years and older – "From twenty years of age and up – everyone who goes out to the legion in Israel..."[157] Thus, the counting process is connected with the idea of counting soldiers in an army.

The following letter is addressed to participants in a convention of N'shei uB'nos Chabad, the Lubavitch women's organization. In this letter, the Rebbe explains that each person who was counted was counted as one person, regardless of his stature in the community. Similarly, each person in God's army, which is comprised of all Jews, is a significant participant in carrying out the overall mission of making the world a dwelling place for God.

The Jewish women of the generation that left Egypt had a decisive role in bringing up the children who would comprise the next generation of God's army. These children were the people who were counted by Moses himself. Similarly, the Jewish wife and mother of our times has a decisive role in raising the next generation of God's army – the generation that will, God willing, be the one that will be redeemed from the current exile through the coming of *Mashiach*.

---

157 Numbers 1:3, *Artscroll Tanach*, Mesorah Publications, Ltd., Brooklyn, New York, 2003

The Rebbe writes:
Likkutei Sichot vol. 18, pp. 423-424

This year's convention is taking place in the days that are connected with Shabbat *Parashat Bamidbar*. Since everything is by Divine Providence, especially an event that is for the benefit of many, we must relate it to the weekly Torah portion and derive instructions from it, for Torah means <u>instruction</u>.

The Torah portion of *Bamidbar* is the beginning of the entire Book of Numbers, which is also called *Sefer Hapikudim* — the Book of Enumerations, because both in the beginning of this Book and at its end, the Torah tells us how the Jews were counted. The first time was in the Desert of Sinai, after receiving the Torah, at the beginning of their long wandering through the vast and frightening desert. The second time was at the end of the forty years of wandering, before their entry into the Land of Israel.

One of the eternal instructions that can be derived from this — because the Torah is eternal and all of its instructions are eternal, for all Jews and for each Jew, at all times and in all places — is:

The soul descends from Heaven to this world with a Godly mission, which every Jew, man or woman, must carry out: to make an abode for God in this material and physical world. When a Jew looks around and sees that the world around him is a spiritual desert, full of materialism and often even lower [spiritually], he may think: "How is it possible to carry out such a mission?"

The Torah tells us that we need not be afraid, for this is the way the Jews began their mission when they became a nation and received the Torah at Mount Sinai. With the strength derived from the Torah, they traversed the vast and frightening desert — a desolate wilderness in all respects, where in the natural order of things there is no bread and no water — a place that is full of difficulties and trials. Moreover, wherever they went, they transformed the desert into a blooming garden — through Miriam's well that caused the desert all around to bring forth all sorts of vegetation and fruit. They brought down "bread from Heaven," the pillar of fire illuminated their path, and the Clouds of Glory protected them from all dangers, etc. — as our Sages explained.

This is also one of the meanings of the [above-mentioned] enumerations, which were conducted in such a way that each one was counted, regardless of his stature and standing in life, and was counted not more and not less than once: to underscore that everyone has his Divine mission as a "soldier" in the ranks of "God's Army," in the service of God. Although in an army there are various ranks, from an ordinary soldier to the highest in rank, each one individually and all of them together carry out the Divine mission to make an abode in this world for God, even in a desert. It was specifically those who were counted in the second enumeration — those who were brought up in the desert — that merited entering the Land of Israel.

Let us again emphasize here the important role of Jewish women and daughters, thanks to whom there were those to be counted in the ranks of "God's Army" — both at the time of the Exodus from Egypt, and at the time of entry into the Land of Israel.

Similarly, in all generations, particularly in the present time, the Jewish wife and mother, and the daughter who is preparing herself for that role, is the *akeret habayit*. As such, she has a decisive role in raising God's "soldiers," with whom we will go out of the present Exile together with our righteous *Mashiach* very soon indeed.

STUDY QUESTIONS:

1. On what two occasions were the Jews counted in the Book of Numbers?

2.   What is the overall purpose of a Jew's life?

3.   Why might someone be intimidated from carrying out this mission?

4.   How can someone strengthen herself from being intimidated by the spiritual desolation of the world?

5.   What is the significance of the fact that people of all different statures were each counted only once?

6.   What was the women's connection to the counting process?

7.   What lesson can today's woman derive from the role that the women played in the counting process?

Parashat Naso

HAIR COVERING FOR MARRIED WOMEN

Parashat Naso describes the commandments related to the *sotah*, who is a woman suspected by her husband of being unfaithful. The husband brings her to the *Beit Hamikdash*, and the *kohen* performs a procedure that is specified in this Torah portion. As part of this procedure, the *kohen* uncovers the woman's hair, thus showing that it is disgraceful for a married Jewish woman to leave her hair exposed.[158] Therefore,[159] Jewish law requires that a married woman cover her hair.

In the following excerpt from a letter, the Rebbe emphasizes the importance of the commandment of hair covering for married women. He explains that this commandment is properly observed by wearing a wig, since kerchiefs and hats do not completely cover the hair. He mentions the great reward that one earns for observing this commandment properly. He then addresses the concern that a woman may be embarrassed to wear a wig because people might make fun of her. She must keep in mind the basic principle underlying the *Code of Jewish Law* (*Shulchan Aruch*) – not to be embarrassed by those who ridicule observance of commandments. In addition, she should fear God, who is always watching her, more than she fears a human being.

---

158 *Rashi's* commentary on Numbers 5:18
159 *Ketubot* 72a

The Rebbe writes:
Likkutei Sichot vol. 13, p. 187

This letter is a reply to her letter in which she writes about wearing a wig, about how those in her religious community do not follow this practice, and about how she is embarrassed and concerned that people may laugh at her if she wears a wig.

In essence, the necessity of wearing a wig, and not sufficing with a hat or kerchief, is explained in various places. It is clearly apparent that wearing a hat, or even a kerchief, leaves part of the hair uncovered (at least for a short while). One thereby transgresses the serious prohibition that is stated in *Shulchan Aruch*, Section *Orach Chaim*, Chapter 75. The magnitude of this issue is understood from the great reward that one receives for fulfilling this commandment according to the way we have been commanded. In the words of the holy *Zohar*, "One is blessed with everything — with blessings from above, with blessings from below, with wealth, with children, and with grandchildren."

Concerning her statement that perhaps people will laugh at her, and she will be embarrassed, and so on:

Even among the youth of the United States, there is lately a feeling of respect, specifically toward those who stand staunchly for their position and are not embarrassed by people who laugh at them and their outlook. In contrast, they relate with ridicule and disdain toward those who follow the majority without any spiritual steadfastness whatsoever. Certainly, she realizes that the teaching at the beginning of all four portions of the *Shulchan Aruch* is that one should not be embarrassed by people who ridicule him for his service of God, blessed be He.[160]

---

160 [*Shulchan Aruch*, 1:1, Rema]

Furthermore, and this is understandable and simple: God, blessed be He, about whom it is written,[161] "I fill the Heaven and the earth," is in a person's presence in <u>all</u> places and at <u>all</u> times. This omnipresence is not applicable to people, not even to a person in one's immediate environment, because he is not always in one's close proximity. Therefore, could it be that someone will not be embarrassed (God forbid) in front of the Holy One, blessed be He, and would be embarrassed in front of a human being made of flesh and blood?!

I hope that there is no need for further elaboration on this topic.

STUDY QUESTIONS:

1. What concern might a married woman have about wearing a wig?

2. What is the deficiency of wearing a kerchief to cover one's hair?

3. What reward does the *Zohar* mention for properly covering one's hair?

4. Toward what type of person does the youth of the United States show the most respect?

5. When a person keeps in mind that God is everywhere, how would he or she feel about acting improperly?

---

161 [Jeremiah 23:24]

Parashat Beha'alotecha

LIGHTING UP THE WORLD

In *Parashat Beha'alotecha*, God commands Aaron, the *Kohen Gadol*, to light the Menorah in the *Beit Hamikdash*. The word used to describe this procedure is *beha'alotecha*, whose literal meaning is "when you bring up." *Rashi* explains that the use of this term indicates that the *Kohen Gadol* must hold a flame to the lamp until the flame on the lamp "comes up," i.e., burns on its own.[162]

In the following letter, addressed to a convention of Nshei uB'nos Chabad, the Rebbe explains that every Jew is a member of the "priestly nation."[163] Therefore, each of us has an obligation to illuminate our surroundings, in a way analogous to the *Kohen Gadol*'s lighting the Menorah, whose light shone not only in the *Beit Hamikdash*, but on the world around it as well. The way a Jew lights up his surroundings in a spiritual way is to first light up his own soul with the fire of Torah. Then, he can share this light of Torah with another Jew, to the point where that Jew is sufficiently lit up that he can shine on his own, and thereby provide spiritual light for others.

The Rebbe then explains that the woman has a special duty and privilege to light up her surroundings, as is evident from the fact that it is she who lights the Shabbat candles in the Jewish home. Thus, she also has the ability and privilege of providing spiritual light for her family and friends, and by extension – to the entire Jewish nation.

---

162 *Rashi*'s commentary on Numbers 8:2
163 Exodus 19:6

The Rebbe writes:
Likkutei Sichot vol. 18, pp. 451-453

This year's convention takes place in the days connected with Shabbat *Parashat Beha'alotecha*. As has been often pointed out we can, and therefore must, derive instructive Torah lessons (Torah means instruction) from the weekly Torah portion that have special relevance to the events and happenings of this particular week.

In the beginning of the Torah portion are the words, "When you light the lamps " — there is a clear instruction that a Jew has to "kindle lights" to illuminate one's surroundings. In this, too, a Jew has to emulate the Creator who, immediately after creating heaven and earth, illuminated it with the order, "Let there be light."

The essential thing about a lamp, in the physical sense, is that it should give light and illuminate its surroundings. An unlit or extinguished lamp brings no benefit, and has no meaning of its own. Only when a lamp gives light and shines does it fulfill its purpose; to provide illumination for a person so that he is able to see what is going on around him, to illuminate his way so that he should not stumble, and to enable him to do and accomplish what he must.

The nature of a lamp is that when one puts a flame to its wick, even a small flame — so long as he does it effectively, the flame catches on and then the lamp begins to give light on its own. This, too, is indicated in the text, "When you light the lamps of the Menorah" — light them until the flame goes up on its own.

The instruction is this:

God gives the human being a soul, a Divine "lamp," as it is written, "A man's soul is the lamp of God"[164] — to illuminate his path in life, and to illuminate the world. But

---

164 [Proverbs 20:27, *Artscroll Tanach*, Mesorah Publications, Ltd., Brooklyn, New York, 2003]

this soul-lamp must first be kindled with the flame of Torah in order that it should shine with its true light, the light of "For a commandment is a lamp and the Torah is light."[165]

This is the task and purpose of every Jew: to be a brightly shining lamp and to kindle, or add brightness to, every Divine "lamp" — Jewish soul — with which one comes into contact. One must do this with completeness, in a way that the lamps they light continue to shine brightly on their own, and so that they also become "lamp-lighters," [kindling other souls,] from candle to candle, in an uninterrupted chain.

It is understood that although the instruction, "When you light [bring up] the lamps," was given to Aaron the *Kohen*, the lesson derived from it is relevant to all Jews, since all Jews are members of the "kingdom of *kohanim*" (i.e., servants of God).[166] Moreover, there is the exhortation: "Be among the disciples of Aaron...loving the creatures and bringing them close to Torah,"[167] to be among the disciples of Aaron, permeated with love of one's fellow Jew, and bringing Jews close to Torah.

If the above pertains to every Jew and all Jews, it is even more emphatically relevant to the Jewish woman, for she is the actual lamp lighter, to whom God gave the special assignment, great privilege, and bright commandment of lighting the candles for the holy Shabbat and *Yom Tov*. The spiritual significance of this is:

In her role as *akeret habayit*, it is her privilege to light up the Jewish home and everyone in her household, which includes her husband, children, and the friends and guests who come into the home as well. In addition, in her role as mother of the children, she is the first to light up the young souls of the infants, until they begin to shine on their own. Thus, she has a very important share in making her Jewish

---

165 [Proverbs 6:23]
166 [Exodus 19:6]
167 [*Pirkei Avot* 1:12]

home, and the House of Israel as a whole — a fitting home for the Divine Presence, in accordance with God's intent and desire — "that I may dwell among (and within) them."

It is superfluous to underscore that in order to fulfill these most important tasks in a maximally complete way, Jewish daughters must be thoroughly prepared with a pure and holy Torah-true education (*al taharat hakodesh*), from the cradle to the wedding. Also later, as *akeret habayit* and mother of children, she must deepen and broaden this Torah education, so that they can illuminate and brighten her Jewish home and the whole House of Israel, with the light and vitality of, "A commandment is a lamp and the Torah is light," in the fullest measure.

STUDY QUESTIONS:

1.   What activity can each Jew do that is analogous to the *Kohen Gadol's* lighting the lamp in the *Beit Hamikdash*?

2.   Why must a lamp be lit in order to be maximally useful?

3.   What is the procedure for using one candle–based lamp to light another one?

4.   What is the spiritual analog of a lamp?

5.   What make the woman especially suited to provide spiritual illumination to those around her?

6.   What must a person do to ensure that his/her lamp is providing the proper type of illumination?

Parashat Shlach

THE LOVE OF WOMEN FOR THE LAND
OF ISRAEL – PHYSICAL AND SPIRITUAL

In *Parashat Shlach,* Moses sent messengers to explore the Land of Israel, which God had promised to give to the Jewish people. These messengers were assigned to report to the rest of the Jews – who were still in the desert – about what they saw. The picture they painted upon their return was grim and frightened the Jews, making many of them not want to enter the Land. However, the women were not scared by the report of the messengers; they remained steadfast in their love for the Land of Israel.

The following letter is addressed to a gathering of friends of the Bais Rivkah School. In this letter, the Rebbe explains a lesson that we can learn from the above-mentioned events from the Torah portion. The women, by remaining steadfast in their love for the Land of Israel, displayed an example to be followed by the women of all succeeding generations.

One way that women of all times and places can show their love for the Land of Israel is by re-creating the spiritual essence of the Holy Land in their own surroundings. Although the Land of Israel is a physical location, a Jew can, to some extent, re-create the holiness of the Land wherever he/she is by living according to the Torah and its commandments. Just as the women of the generation of the desert had a love for the Land of Israel that was so powerful that they could ignore the bad reports of the messengers, the women of all times and places have a special ability and responsibility to re-create the holiness of the Land of Israel in their own homes.

The Rebbe writes:
Likkutei Sichot vol. 23 pp. 359-360

By Divine Providence, this year's gathering occurs the day after the Shabbat of *Parashat Shlach*. According to a Jewish custom, and specifically according to the statement of the *Alter Rebbe* that "A Jew must live with the time," we find in this Torah portion a lesson that has a special relevance to all participants in this gathering of friends of Bais Rivkah.

The content of the Torah portion, which is indicated in its name, is the well-known story about the spies who were sent to bring a first-hand report from the land that God designated as an eternal inheritance of the Jewish nation, and [regarding which He] was prepared to fulfill His promise that He made while the Jews were still in exile in Egypt — "I will bring you to the Land... "[168] — to lead the Jews into the Land of Israel.

In connection with these events, it is well known that the Jewish women of that generation again (just like they did earlier at the Giving of the Torah and at the building of the *Mishkan*, etc.) displayed a splendid example for the entire Jewish nation: the women did <u>not</u> listen to the misleading words of the spies. On the contrary, the women displayed a very strong love of the Land of Israel, and, as the Torah recounts about the daughters of Tzelofchad, demanded and received a portion in the Holy Land, etc.

Thus, the women of that generation also set an example for Jewish women and daughters in all future generations, because the lessons derived from the stories in the Torah, like all the lessons from the Torah — the Torah of life (instruction on life) — are eternal for all times and places.

The statement of the Rebbe, the *Tzemach Tzedek*, is well known, that <u>a Jew has the capability</u> — in a spiritual sense — <u>to create "the Land of Israel" wherever he is</u>, beginning with his own home and neighborhood. The unique quality of the

---

168 [Exodus 6:8]

Land of Israel is its holiness, which is connected with the Divine Presence, and especially the Divine Providence in the Land, as the Torah describes, "The eyes of the L-rd, your God, are always upon it, from the beginning of the year until the end of the year"[169] — always, without interruption.

Therefore, when a Jew conducts his day-to-day life in accordance with God's will, and the home is permeated with the light and holiness of Torah and its commandments, then his environment is "the Land of Israel" in the spiritual sense.

STUDY QUESTIONS:

1.　　What promise did God make to the Jewish people while they were still slaves in Egypt?

2.　　How did the women react to the misleading report of the spies on the Land of Israel?

3.　　What strong feeling did the women have that enabled them to maintain the proper attitude regarding the Land of Israel?

4.　　What lesson can we draw for our own lives from these women's example?

5.　　What is the unique feature of the Land of Israel?

6.　　How can we make our own environment analogous to the Land of Israel?

---

169 [Deuteronomy 11:12]

Parashat Korach

THE TREMENDOUS INFLUENCE OF THE WIFE

Parashat Korach tells the story of Korach, a close relative of Moses from the tribe of Levi. Korach challenged the leadership of Moses. His argument was that all Jews are holy, so why should Moses have a special role as the leader of the Jewish nation? Korach gathered hundreds of people to join him in his challenge to Moses.

Moses tried to convince Korach of the lack of validity of his argument, but Korach persisted. As a result, Korach and his followers were killed by God in extraordinary ways. However, one of Korach's followers, On ben Pelet, withdrew from Korach's group and was thereby saved.

In the following letter addressed to a group of women, the Rebbe discusses the story of Korach and On, as described in the *Gemara* and *Midrashim*. He points out that the totally opposite outcomes that befell Korach and On were due to the influence of their wives. Korach's wife encouraged him to challenge Moses, while On's wife convinced him to withdraw from Korach's group. Thus, the woman has a tremendous influence on the well-being of her husband and family. This comes with a great responsibility to use this influence in the best way.

The Rebbe writes:
Likkutei Sichot vol. 2, pp. 689-690

At this opportunity, I would also like to underscore and call attention to the story, which is told in the Torah portion that we have just read in the Torah — *Parashat Korach*. This story must serve as an instructive lesson for every Jew in general, for women specifically, and especially for the women and girls of Chabad, whom the holy Rebbes demand to conduct themselves beyond the letter of the law in love of God, love of one's fellow Jew, and love of the Torah, and they give them the capability to do so.

Here is the story and its instructive lesson:

Korach was one of the elite Jews — he was a descendant of one of the finest families. He was a great scholar, one of the wealthiest men, a very intelligent man, and a close relative of Moses our Rabbi and Aaron the *Kohen*. In contrast, On ben Pelet, one of Korach's followers, does not seem to be at all distinguished: not in wisdom, not in family ancestry, and not in other areas.

How did their lives turn out?

Exactly the opposite of the way we would have expected.

Korach had a desolate end, and he dragged hundreds and hundreds of Jews into misfortune with him.

On ben Pelet, by contrast, was saved together with his whole family. He was the <u>one and only</u> person who was not punished from among all of those who were in Korach's group.

What is the explanation for such an unexpectedly bad outcome for Korach and such a good one for On ben Pelet?

<u>The influence and conduct of their wives!</u>

The wife of On ben Pelet, albeit in the final hours before Korach and his followers perished, saved her husband and their whole family through her influence. She was a true *akeret habayit*.

Korach's wife, on the other hand, contributed through her words and conduct to her husband's downfall and to the downfall of his whole group. Instead of being the *akeret habayit*, the foundation of the home, she was the *okeret*[170] *habayit*, the one who uprooted the home.

This story is told in detail in Gemara[171] and *Midrashim*.

All this must repeatedly bring each one of us to contemplate deeply the immense responsibility of a woman and the extremely important role that she has in the good and the well-being of her husband and family.

As King Solomon says, "The wisdom of women" — the wise conduct of women — "has built her home"[172] — builds the well-being of her home. In the opposite situation, events turn out, God forbid, in the way that the verse describes further.

STUDY QUESTIONS:

1. What was the family background of Korach?

2. What were several good qualities of Korach?

3. What do we know about the type of person On ben Pelet was?

4. What kind of influence did Korach's wife and On's wife have on their husbands in connection with joining in Korach's argument?

---

170 [The word *okeret* means "one who uproots." This word's Hebrew root is similar to that of the word *akeret*, which means "foundation" when used in the phrase a*keret habayit*.]
171 *Sanhedrin* 109b
172 Proverbs 14:1

5.   What conclusion can a Jewish woman draw regarding
      her responsibility to influence her family?

Parashat Chukat

MAKING TORAH ACCESSIBLE
TO EVEN THE YOUNGEST

Parashat Chukat recounts the passing of Miriam. It was in Miriam's merit that the Jews had the Well of Miriam, which was their source of water during their travels through the desert. When she passed away, the well disappeared, and only after Moses prayed to God was their source of water restored.

In the following excerpts, the Rebbe explains the special significance of water, and what Miriam did that made her merit to help provide the Jews with water. The nature of water is that it comes from a high place down to a low place. Similarly, Miriam made the Torah, which comes from God – the highest place of all – accessible to even the youngest children.

The stories in the Torah, as well as the commandments, provide instruction to us on how to conduct ourselves in our lives. The way that Miriam made the Torah accessible to even the young children – those who know very little about Torah – is an example for us to emulate in our own lives.

The Rebbe writes:
Likkutei Sichot[173] vol. 2, pp. 331-335

In teachings of our Sages on themes in *Parashat Chukat*, we find Clouds of Glory attributed to the merit of Aaron, the Well (of water) to the merit of Miriam, and *manna* to the merit

---

173 The following translation (including the footnotes) is based on the English translation of the discourse, from the book entitled *Likkutei Sichot*, translated by Rabbi Jacob Immanuel Schochet, Kehot Publication Society, 1992. Some sections of the discourse are omitted here; the location of these sections is indicated by "..."

of Moses. The Clouds of Glory and the Well disappeared with the passing of Aaron and Miriam, but were then restored in the merit of Moses.

The Torah embodies wisdom, as it is said, "For it is your wisdom and understanding in the eyes of the nations."[174] Nonetheless, it is not referred to as Wisdom, but as Torah, an expression of *hora'ah* (instruction, teaching). For everything in the Torah is an instruction for day-to-day life, at all times and in all places.

In other words, not only the commandments (the positive and negative precepts) in the Torah, but the narratives in the Torah, too, provide instructions for life. Indeed, even the commandments themselves are not recorded in the Torah as direct commands, but appear in narrative contexts: God spoke to Moses, and then Moses related this to the Jewish people. Thus, just as the commandments are instructions, notwithstanding the fact that they are related in narrative form, so also the narratives in the Torah are instructions, for they too are an integral part of the Torah.

Maimonides thus writes — and this is already alluded to in the Gemara[175] — that there is no difference between a verse like "And the sister of Lotan was Timna,"[176] and the verse "Hear O Israel..."[177] The verse "Hear O Israel" does indeed teach one of the fundamental precepts of the Torah, while the verse, "And the sister of Lotan..." is merely a narrative. Even so, both are narratives, both offer instructions, and both represent the Divine wisdom and will.

As all narratives in the Torah offer instructions for life, this applies also to the narrative referred to above.

---

174 Deuteronomy 4:6
175 *Sanhedrin* 99b
176 Genesis 36:22
177 Deuteronomy 6:4

The three concepts of Clouds of Glory, the *manna*, and the Well, all of which are found in the Torah, are readily understood.

The Clouds of Glory offered protection against anything from the outside. They protected from all four directions, killed the snakes in the desert and leveled mountainous terrain. Furthermore, they kept the Israelites' garments clean and neat, as it is said, "Your garments did not wear out."[178] All these are aspects of protection from the outside.

The *manna* is something edible, and it assumed any taste desired by those who ate it. Edibles are things that are taken in, something related to within.

The Well is water. Water per se is not a nutriment. That is why an *eiruv*[179] cannot be effected with water, as Maimonides explains, because an *eiruv* can be effected only with food, and water is not regarded as food. However, the function of water is to move the food to all parts of the body.

These three concepts apply to Torah as well: there is the concept of Torah being effective from within; the concept of Torah protecting from the outside; and the concept of the Torah carrying over these two aspects to all Jews.

* * *

In order for a Jew to bring out the Torah-dimensions of the *manna* and the Clouds of Glory, one needs to have the Water-aspect of Torah. Waters descend from a higher plane to a lower one. It is likewise with the Torah; it descended to, and became invested in, the lower world — beautiful wisdom in an ugly vessel. By virtue of this lowering of the Torah, every Jew can bring out the Torah-dimensions of the *manna* and the

---

178 Deuteronomy 8:4

179 [The word "*eiruv*" in this context may refer to an "*eiruv tavshilin.*" This phrase literally means, "mixing of cooked dishes." It is an arrangement whereby one prepares a cooked food prior to a Jewish holiday that will be followed by the Shabbat, for the purpose of allowing one to prepare food for Shabbat on the holiday, which would otherwise be prohibited.]

Clouds of Glory when reciting the *Written Torah* (even if he does not understand the meaning of the words), or learning the *Oral Torah* (even if he understands no more than its simple meaning).

Just as water transports the food to all parts of the body, so too does the Water of the Torah. As the Torah descended and became invested below, it carries the *manna* of the Torah and the Clouds of Glory of the Torah throughout the camp of Israel, to every Jewish man and woman, with respect to all of their needs.

* * *

Miriam is identified with Pu'ah, who took care of the little children in Egypt and helped raise them. She was named Miriam because she was born when the harshness of the exile became more severe[180], yet she prophesied that the savior of Israel was about to be born. Thus, she negated not only the decree of Pharaoh but also that of Amram, notwithstanding the fact that Amram had a good reason for his decree.[181] She proceeded with self-sacrifice to raise children who would say, "This is my God, and I will praise Him,"[182] a generation that would receive the Torah. The Well — water — thus came by her virtue; for water signifies bringing the Torah to a lowly place, and dispersing it to those who are at the very end of the camp.

STUDY QUESTIONS:

1. What means of sustenance did the Jews in the desert have in the merit of Miriam?

---

180 [The name "Miriam" is related to the Hebrew word *mar*, which means "bitter",]

181 [Amram, Miriam's father, was the greatest of his generation. When Pharaoh decreed the death of male children, Amram divorced his wife, and all Israelites followed his example. Miriam then rebuked him: "Your decree is worse than Pharaoh's; for Pharaoh decreed only against the males, while you have decreed against the males and the females..." Amram acknowledged the validity of Miriam's argument, and remarried his wife, who then gave birth to Moses, the redeemer of Israel (*Rashi's* commentary on Exodus 2:1).]

182 [Exodus 15:2]

2. How can narratives in the Torah serve as instructions for us to follow?

3. What is the function of water in the human body, and what is the analog to that in the connection between a Jew and the Torah?

4. What is the "water-aspect" of Torah?

5. What did Miriam do to bring the teachings of Torah to many Jews?

Parashat Balak

DILIGENT OBSERVANCE OF THE PRINCIPLES
OF MODEST CONDUCT

In *Parashat Balak*, King Balak of Moab hired Bilam, a master magician, to bring curses upon the Jews. Bilam prepared to utter these curses, but God performed a miracle and brought words of blessing from his mouth instead.

In one of Bilam's blessings, he praised the arrangement of the Jews' tents, which were grouped separately, according to tribe. Also, within each group, the doors of the tents were not situated directly opposite each other, so that no one would be able to look inside his neighbor's tent.

In the following excerpts from a discourse, the Rebbe discusses some of *Rashi*'s explanations of the verses concerning Bilam's blessing. The Rebbe explains that one must be careful about even seemingly minor aspects of principles of modest conduct. Diligent observance of these principles has a powerful positive effect – even to the point of transforming the evil intentions of a master magician into blessings.

To make the Rebbe's discussion easier to understand, translations[183] of the relevant verses and *Rashi*'s explanations of them are given here:

Numbers, Chapter 24, verse 2:

> *And Bilam lifted up his eyes and he saw Israel dwelling tribe by tribe; and there came upon him the spirit of God.*

---

183 Translation is based on *The Pentateuch and Rashi's Commentary; A Linear Translation into English* by Rabbi Abraham ben Isaiah and Rabbi Benjamin Sharfman, S.S.&R. Publishing Co., Brooklyn, NY, 1950

Rashi on "dwelling tribe by tribe":

> *He saw each tribe dwelling by itself, and that they are not intermixed. He saw that their doors were not directed one opposite the other, lest one look into the tent of his fellow man.*

Rashi on "and there came upon him the spirit of God":

> *It entered his heart that he should not curse them.*

Numbers, Chapter 24, verses 3-4:

> *And he took up his parable and said: "The saying of Bilam the son of Beor, and the saying of the man whose eye is opened; the saying of him who hears the words of God, who sees the vision of the Almighty, fallen down, yet with opened eyes:"*

Numbers, Chapter 24, verse 5:

> *How goodly are your tents, O Jacob, your dwellings, O Israel.*

Rashi on "How goodly are your tents":

> *Because he saw that their doors were not directed one opposite the other.*

The Rebbe writes:
Likkutei Sichot vol. 13, pp. 83-84

The lesson from the above-mentioned explanations of *Rashi*:

The content of his explanation shows the importance of the idea of modesty. The fact that "their doors were not directed one opposite the other" is apparently not a fundamental principle of modesty, because its purpose was simply so that "one would not look into the tent of his fellow man." Nevertheless, even this observance had the power to bring about the fact that even for the wicked Bilam: "It entered his heart that he not curse them," and he even blessed them: "...stretching out like brooks..."[184]

The lesson from this is: a person should not say that regarding a major and fundamental principle in modesty — such as the fact that "Each tribe dwelled by itself, <u>and they were not intermixed</u>" — he will be scrupulous, but regarding a minute detail, it is not necessary to be so particular. He must realize that even this detail is a fundamental principle, to the extent that it has the power to transform every undesirable matter from one extreme to its opposite extreme.

There is still room for temptation by the evil inclination, which says: "All of the above is applicable to a permanent manner of conduct, but when the subject is a temporary manner of conduct, it is not obligatory to be so particular about modesty, and to be as careful about minute details as about major issues."

[The following was written by the Rebbe as a footnote, and the published version of this discourse, which was edited by him, shows it in large, bold letters:] **Here is the place to emphasize a timely issue: There are those who are "lenient" on several aspects of modesty in the summer, and particularly those who are living in temporary residences outside the city. Among them are those who say: "I will sin and I will repent — when I return to the city."**

This is also relevant to men, and particularly to women, for each one of them is called *akeret habayit.* **It is possible to discuss this at length, but this is not the place to do so.**

There is an instruction that responds to this argument: "He saw that their doors were not directed one opposite the other" — even when they were dwelling in tents, "<u>your tents,</u> O Jacob " Such a level of scrupulousness and modesty is applicable even in a temporary "tent."

---

184 [Numbers 24:6. This phrase is the continuation of the blessing in the previous verse.]

On the other hand, when one is scrupulous in this matter, then God's conduct is in a manner of "How <u>goodly</u> are your tents, O Jacob, your dwellings, O Israel" — then "the L-rd your God <u>reversed</u>..."[185] This verse describes how God reversed Bilam's curse into a blessing. And as *Rashi* explains the next verse,[186] "He intended...but when God reversed his words, he blessed them..." Bilam even mentioned the promise of the *Mishkan* in its completeness — that the Holy One, blessed be He shall return the *mashkon* (pledge) — the eternal dwelling place. The term *mashkon* indicates that even while it is destroyed, it still exists, and when the atonement is completed, it will descend and be revealed, forever and ever.

STUDY QUESTIONS:

1. What positive result came about due to the fact that the door of the Jews' tents in the desert did not face each other?

2. Does observance of minute details of the principles of modest conduct have a significant effect? If so, what is an example of this?

3. How do we know from the *parsha* that even a temporary lapse in modest conduct is not acceptable?

4. What is one setting in which it is particularly tempting to conduct oneself immodestly?

5. What is the greatest blessing with which Bilam blessed the Jews?

---

185 Deuteronomy 23:6
186 [Numbers 24:6]

Parashat Pinchas

HAPPY IS THE PERSON WHOSE WORDS
GOD ACKNOWLEDGES

In *Parashat Pinchas*, God tells Moses the laws of dividing the Land of Israel among the families of the Jewish nation. Among the details is that only sons inherit their father's portion of land.

The Torah here relates the story of a man named Tzelofchad, who had only daughters and no sons. Tzelofchad's daughters were concerned that their father's children would receive no portion in the Land of Israel. They respectfully approached Moses and asked him to grant them a portion in the Land. Moses did not feel competent to answer their question, and asked God what to do. God answered that the daughters of Tzelofchad had a proper claim. God then told Moses the laws of inheritance for the case in which a man has no sons. The daughters of Tzelofchad were thus granted a portion in the Land of Israel.

In the following excerpt, the Rebbe quotes *Rashi's* comment on God's answer to Moses, "They claimed correctly. Fortunate is the person whose words the Holy One, blessed be He, acknowledges."[187] The Rebbe explains that the request of the daughters of Tzelofchad to inherit a portion in the Land of Israel showed their great love of the Land. It was in the merit of this great love that some of the laws of inheritance were revealed through them. Also, because of their high spiritual level, God acknowledged the validity of their words. Similarly, all Jewish women have the ability – when they

---

187 *Rashi's* commentary on Numbers 27:7, *The Pentateuch and Rashi's Commentary, A Linear Translation into English* by Rabbi Abraham ben Isaiah and Rabbi Benjamin Sharfman; S.S. & R. Publishing Company; Brooklyn, NY, 1977

express the true essence of their soul – to attain a spiritual level at which God, as it were, acknowledges the truth of their words.

Note: Excerpts from the continuation of this discourse are presented in the sections for *Parashat Metzora* (page 151) and *Parashat Shemini* (page 137).

The Rebbe writes:
Likkutei Sichot, vol. 13, pp. 256-257

The fourth reading in today's Torah portion begins with God telling Moses: "The daughters of Tzelofchad speak correctly." The meaning of this statement is as *Rashi* explains, "They claimed <u>correctly</u>," i.e., God <u>praises</u> them and supports their claim. *Rashi* concludes by stating, "Happy is the person whose words God acknowledges."

This section of *Parashat Pinchas*, which expresses the importance and wisdom of the daughters of Tzelofchad and the correctness of their demand to have an inheritance in the Land of Israel, is a continuation of the previous section (the third reading), in which the Torah underscores the merit of the daughters of Israel by comparison with the sons of Israel:

They, the daughters of Israel, loved the Land of Israel. They were of the opinion that "The Land is very, very good,"[188] despite the fact that at that time, there was room for a misguided opposition to coming and serving God in the Land of Israel. This opposition was based on the hope that what is required is the service of "the World of Thought " or "the World of Speech" (which were the main types of service during the time in the desert), and not the lowering of oneself to the service of the "World of <u>Action</u>" — the main service in the Land of Israel.

---

188 Numbers 14:7

This very virtue of the daughters of Israel is expressed in the story of the daughters of Tzelofchad. They specifically demanded, "Give us a possession," in contrast to the claim, "Let us appoint a leader and return [to Egypt]."[189] As a result, although this section with its laws should have been said by Moses, the daughters of Tzelofchad merited that it was written through them, as *Rashi* cites in his commentary.[190]

The lesson that the Torah teaches us in this Torah portion is comprehensible even by a five-year-old boy, and by a girl — it is possible to say — at an even younger age, since an additional measure of understanding was granted to women, the reason why a girl becomes obligated to observe the commandments at a younger age than does a boy.

This lesson is, like all lessons in the Torah, an eternal Torah instruction for all times and places. The Torah teaches us how great is the power and merit of Jewish women and girls. It shows how much they can achieve when they reveal in themselves the true nature of the Jewish soul, the Godly spark that originates from the highest spiritual levels. They can then accomplish that God <u>acknowledges</u> their words — such that God agrees with their words in a manner of acknowledgement, as it were. This follows the model of, "A righteous person decrees and God fulfills [the person's decree]."[191]

STUDY QUESTIONS:

1. What was the request of the daughters of Tzelofchad, which God praised them for?

2. What was the erroneous attitude toward living in the Land of Israel which some people felt at that time?

---

189 Numbers 14:4
190 *Rashi's* commentary on Numbers 27:5
191 *Midrash Tanchuma*, *Parashat Vayeira* 19, [and other references cited in the original text of this discourse.]

3.   How was the attitude of Tzelofchad's daughters different from this erroneous attitude?

4.   What is one reward that God gave the daughters of Tzelofchad in response to their request?

5.   What lesson can we derive from this incident with the daughters of Tzelofchad?

Parashat Matot

THE TREMENDOUS VALUE OF
SERVING GOD THROUGH INVOLVEMENT
WITH THE PHYSICAL WORLD

In *Parashat Matot*, there is a section about the laws of vows. In particular, a father can annul his daughter's vows and a husband can annul his wife's vows. However, this law applies only to vows concerning abstaining from enjoying some physical item.[192]

In the following excerpt from a discourse, the Rebbe cites two opposite concepts regarding the value of vows. An advantage of vows is that they help one distance oneself from sinning. On the other hand, one should not withdraw from being involved with the physical world. After all, the reason we are in this world is to make it a Godly place. The middle path between these two poles is that vows are of value to one who feels prone to sin, but one who can act properly should not make vows. Furthermore, one who annuls a vow actually elevates the one who made the vow from the lower level of being someone who needs to make a vow to the higher level of someone who need not and should not make a vow.

The Rebbe points out that these laws were given to the Jews at the time when they were in the desert and about to enter the Land of Israel. In the desert, their service to God required very little involvement with the physical world, since their material needs were miraculously provided for by God. However, this manner of service was appropriate only for the temporary period of their trip through the desert. In

---

192 Also, a husband may annul vows that his wife makes that may negatively affect their relationship.

the Land of Israel, they would serve God in the way that He always intended– through involvement with the physical world. Thus, both the annulment of vows and the entry into the Land of Israel share the feature of elevating a person to the level of serving God within the physical world.

It is interesting to note that among the generation about to go into the Holy Land, it was the women who were the most eager to enter and serve God through involvement with the physical world. The men, however, were afraid that this manner of serving G–d would lower their spiritual level (see the chapter on *Parashat Devarim,* page 219). The Rebbe's discussion below about vows shows the tremendous importance and value of serving God through involvement with the physical world.

The Rebbe writes:
Likkutei Sichot vol. 13, pp. 107-109

The statement in the Jerusalem Talmud concerning vows is well known: "Is it not sufficient what the Torah has forbidden you that you seek to forbid yourself other things as well?"[193] The reason for this negative attitude toward vows is understood: the supreme intention for the existence of the Torah and the commandments is to make, by means of them, a dwelling place in this lowest world for Him, blessed be He. Therefore, it is understood that the service of God must be with the material things in the world, to make from them a dwelling place for Him — may He be blessed — and not to distance oneself and be separated from them through vows and oaths.

On the other hand, however, the Sages have stated, "Vows are a safeguard for separateness,"[194] i.e., vows facilitate

---

193 *Nedarim* Chapter 9, Halacha 1
194 *Pirkei Avot* 3:13

the fulfillment of the command, "Sanctify yourself with what is permitted to you."[195]

The distinction between these two instructions is explained by the Rabbis. Concerning a person who conducts himself in a good and proper way, the Sages have stated, "It is sufficient for you what the Torah has forbidden." On the contrary, he is forbidden to make vows since they prevent him from working with and refining the material things. This is not the case with one whose conduct is not completely proper, for in his condition there is a concern that the material matters will bring him to a lower level. About such a person the Sages have said, "Vows are a safeguard for abstinence."

According to this, it is understood that the ultimate goal is to elevate oneself to a level that has an additional advantage, i.e., negation and nullification of the vow. From this, it follows that when the Torah hints that there is some aspect of vows that is relevant specifically to an individual expert (or to three laymen; such a group constitutes a Court) because of his high level — it is understood that the Torah is not talking about fulfillment of the vows, but rather about the nullification and cancellation of the vows. That is, the expert (or the Court) brings about an elevation in the person who vows, to the extent that he reaches a level at which he does not need vows.

According to what was mentioned above, that the main idea of this section of the Torah portion is the cancellation of vows, the reason for the placement of this section on vows next to the account of the entry into the Land of Israel will be understood:

The main difference between the service of the Jewish nation in the desert and their service in the Land of Israel is that in the desert they were not involved with material

---

195 [That is, when you deal with things that are permitted to you, do it in a holy way.]

matters. They were nourished there with "bread from Heaven" (*manna*), they drank water from the Well of Miriam, and they did not need to be concerned with their supply of clothing because their clothing grew along with them. In contrast, in the Land of Israel, they had to be involved with the labors of plowing and sowing, etc. It is specifically this service which, as mentioned above, is the supreme intention: to make a dwelling place for Him, blessed be He, <u>in this lowest world</u>.

Therefore, when they were about to enter the Land of Israel and be involved there with this service, the section on cancellation of vows was mentioned to them, because its inner meaning is also serving God with material matters, as mentioned above.

However, since the actual law of vows is written in this Torah portion — and it was also mentioned to them close to the time of their entry into the Land of Israel and their involvement with material matters — it is understood that this too has in it a lesson regarding this type of service [i.e., serving God through involvement with the physical world].

The main idea of vows is: "He shall not desecrate his word,"[196] i.e., "He shall not make his words profane."[197] This is the manner of service with material matters: to cause his material "things"[198] not to be "profane," but rather to infuse them with holiness.

Since this lesson is hinted in the context of vows themselves, it is understood that <u>each and every person</u> has the ability to perform this service — including someone who has not achieved the level of being able to cancel vows. The reason for this is written further on in the section concerning

---

196 [Numbers 30:3]

197 [The *Midrash*'s interpretation of this phrase, cited in *Rashi*'s commentary on the phrase.]

198 [The Hebrew word in the original text is *devarav*, which could mean "his words" or "his things."]

vows: "Between a man and his wife and between a father and his daughter."[199] Each and every Jew is comparable to a "wife" of God, and a "daughter" of God, and God certainly gives him the ability to perform this service and to fulfill His will to make for Him, blessed be He, a dwelling place in this lowest world.

STUDY QUESTIONS:

1. What drawback is there to making vows?

2. What advantage is there to making vows, and what kind of person is helped by making vows?

3. What effect does a Court's nullification of a person's vow have on that person?

4. What is the inner meaning of the Jews' entrance into the Land of Israel as well as of the cancellation of vows?

5. What lesson can a Jew draw from the concept of nullification of vows in his/her service of God in the role of "wife" or "daughter" of God?

---

199 [Numbers 30:17]

Parashat Mas'ei

In *Parashat Mas'ei*, some of the elders of the tribe of Menasheh, the tribe of Tzelofchad's daughters (see the chapter on *Parashat Pinchas*, page 205), approached Moses with a question: What if the daughters of Tzelofchad marry men from tribes other than their own? Then their sons would not belong to the tribe of Menasheh, and the land they inherit would become the property of a different tribe. Moses answered that the daughters of Tzelofchad – as well as any daughter that inherits land from her father – must marry men from their own tribe. Then the land would continue to belong to the original tribe.

From this story we see that at the time of the events described above, the daughters of Tzelofchad were not yet married. Furthermore, they were almost forty years old. They were still unmarried at that age because until then, they could not find anyone suitable for them.[200] They had voluntarily chosen to live alone rather than lower their spiritual standards by marrying people below their level.[201] They must have had a great trust in God that He would eventually provide them with worthy spouses.

In the following excerpt from a discourse, the Rebbe advises Jewish daughters who are not yet married. He tells them that they must have a complete trust in God, and that He will help them succeed in building a new Jewish home. At the same time, they must make efforts of their own toward this goal. However, their trust in God, and resulting peace of

---

200 *Bamidbar Rabbah* and *Rashi*, cited in *The Midrash Says*, Book of Bamidbar, p. 371 by Rabbi Moses Weissman, Bnei Yakov Publications, 1983.
201 Ibid., p. 376.

mind, will help bring them extraordinary success in their efforts.

The Rebbe writes:
Likkutei Sichot vol. 12, p. 252

Jewish daughters prepare themselves, with God's help and blessings, to build their own homes. These homes should be houses of *kohanim* and houses of kings[202] — like a royal home that is free of worries, and a priestly home, i.e., a holy home. To be an *akeret habayit* for her own Jewish home, the Jewish daughter must be full of trust in God, in the great King who watches over each and every one with Divine Providence, that He will grant her wish. When one relies on the true Master of the world, "Cast upon God your burden,"[203] then there is no place at all for worries.

It is actually true that one must take action according to the natural order of the world. It is necessary to have the approach of "the labor of your hands,"[204] using one's physical body. However, since one feels that God attends to every detail of life, this feeling brings about a true tranquility of the soul and tranquility of the body, a truly calm and good life even on the material level. The statement, "Happy are you in this world"[205] is fulfilled, and one can then devote oneself to truly Jewish matters, and do so with a calm heart and good health, with gladness and goodness of heart. All this causes the success to be incomparably greater than what would be expected from the toil and effort that one exerted.

---

202 As it was stated to each and every Jew: 'And you shall be for Me a kingdom of *kohanim*' (Exodus 19:6).
203 Psalms 55:23
204 Psalms 128:2
205 *Pirkei Avot* 4:1

Study Questions:

1. The Jewish home is compared to what type of home, with what characteristics?

2. What feeling must the Jewish daughter feel about becoming an *akeret habyit* for her own home?

3. What should the Jewish daughter remind herself of in order to not have any worries?

4. What else is necessary for the Jewish daughter to feel and/or do in addition to having trust in God?

5. What is the result, in practical terms, of having trust in God?

Parashat Devarim

Transforming the Material World into a Godly Place

In *Parashat Devarim*, Moses began one of his last speeches to the Jewish nation, which he delivered several weeks before his passing. In the beginning of this speech, he reviewed the history of the Jews' travels through the desert, and rebuked them for the misdeeds that they committed during this time period.

One of the events upon which he dwelled at length is the story of the messengers that he sent to explore the Land of Israel. Most of these messengers came back with a frightening report. The Jewish men became discouraged about going into the Land and complained bitterly. In his speech, Moses rebuked the people for their lack of faith in God. Having experienced the many miracles God performed for them during their travels through the desert, they should have had faith that He would safely bring them into the Holy Land.

In a discourse, part of which is presented below, the Rebbe explains that the reason the men were discouraged was that they enjoyed the spiritual life in the desert. They were afraid that they would not be able to maintain such a high spiritual level in the Land of Israel, where they would have to be involved with material aspects of life such as farming.

The Rebbe also criticizes the attitude that some men may have nowadays – that they would prefer to remain in the spiritual environment of the yeshiva, synagogue or their own home. They are reluctant to deal with the outside world and transform it into a place of Godliness. The Rebbe points out that in Moses' generation, the women were not frightened about going into the Land of Israel. They were actually eager to enter the Land and live in it. Similarly, women today should set an example of an eagerness to be involved with the material world and transform it into a place of Godliness.

The Rebbe writes:
Likkutei Sichot vol.8, pp. 293-294

Our Sages tell us: Whom did the spies influence to feel regret and not want to enter a settled land? It was only the men. As *Rashi* explains[206] , the daughters of Israel, the Jewish women, were not frightened by the report of the spies. Without heeding the attitude of the men, the women said that they were not afraid. They said: If God wants to put us to a test, we should do it right away, even if it temporarily "tears us away," such as that the time we must spend on plowing, sowing, and dealing with non-Jews, time we will not be able to use for learning Torah and performing its commandments.

This is a lesson for the present time as well: We see that there are, unfortunately, many men who feel — as long as they are in yeshiva or in synagogue for praying or attending a Torah lesson – an enthusiasm, ardor and liveliness about not being influenced by what is going on in the outside world. They feel that when they go into the outside world, <u>there</u> they will carry out God's mission. However, when they do go into the outside world, they undergo a transformation, a weakening. The person, nevertheless, is a sincere Jew — he wants to run back into the synagogue and the yeshiva — yet by doing so, he shows that he does not want to occupy himself with making the world into a dwelling place for God, so that Godliness would be apparent also in the outside world.

Just like in those generations, in our generation the women must also show by example that what the spies said

---

206 *Rashi's* commentary on Numbers 26:64

about there being difficult tests and a difficult battle — even though the spies spoke the truth, and told it like it is — has no relevance to the decision to carry out the mission. That is because it is God's mission that Godliness should be apparent not only in the synagogue, Torah study hall and in one's own home, but it should also be apparent wherever a Jew can reach and bring God's word, and carry out God's mission of making that place a dwelling place for God in this lowly world.

STUDY QUESTIONS:

1. What were some frightening aspects of entering the Land of Israel?

2. Why were the Jewish women in the desert not afraid to enter the Land of Israel?

3. In the present time, in which environment is it easiest to carry out God's mission?

4. What relevance does the difficulty in carrying out God's mission in the outside world have on the necessity of doing so?

5. In which environments should God's mission be carried out?

6. What can Jewish women do to ensure that God's mission is carried out wherever it needs to be?

Parashat Vaetchanan

MEZUZOT PROTECT THE JEWISH HOME

Parashat Vaetchanan contains the first paragraph of the *Shema*, a passage that is recited several times daily. One of the commandments mentioned in the *Shema* is the commandment of *mezuzah*. According to the laws of this commandment, a scroll on which are written certain paragraphs from the Torah must be affixed to almost every doorway in a Jewish home.[207]

The following letter was written by the Rebbe to all Jewish women and girls. It was composed in the summer of 1976, shortly after the Arab hijacking of an airplane with many Jews on it to Uganda. In this letter, the Rebbe stresses the importance of ensuring the safety and security of the Jewish home. True security can only be achieved by bringing God's protection to the home. When every aspect of the conduct of the home is in accordance with God's will, He will grant this protection, as expressed in the commandments of the Torah.

However, our Sages have taught us that, of all the commandments, observance of the commandment of *mezuzah* has a special power to bring protection to the home. Furthermore, as described in this letter, one Jew's observance of this commandment increases the security of Jews everywhere. Since the woman is the *akeret habayit*, the foundation of the home in the spiritual sense, she has a special responsibility regarding the observance of this commandment – to ensure that this commandment is

---

207 The laws of this commandment are many and complex, and therefore a Torah-observant rabbi should be consulted regarding proper placement of *mezuzot* in the home.

observed properly in her own home, as well as in the homes of other Jews.

The Rebbe writes:
Likkutei Sichot vol. 14, pp. 203-204

In conjunction with recent events — the capture and the release of the captives in Uganda, as well as the incident of seeking revenge (God forbid) in Kushta (Istanbul) – and as a follow up to them:

We must understand that these events are a reminder that Jews must strengthen their safety and protection as soon as possible, beginning with safety in spiritual life. This brings God's blessing to know what one must do according to the natural order and to do it with much success, in conjunction with God's promise: "God will bless you in everything you do,"[208] in order to be protected and safeguarded against enemies and kept safe from all undesirable events, God forbid.

This reminds all Jews and each Jew, especially Jewish women and girls — keeping in mind that every married Jewish woman is called *akeret habayit,* and those who are yet unmarried must prepare themselves from the youngest age to take their place as an *akeret habayit* — the following:

In the present time in particular, every Jewish house must have protection. The true protection is, as the verse states, "God will guard the city."[209] In order to ensure that God guards the house, all aspects of the conduct of the house must be in accordance with God's will.

Then, the house is also a dwelling place for God's presence, as God has told us in the Torah, "I will dwell among them."[210]

208 [Deuteronomy 15:18]
209 [Paraphrase of Psalms 127:1]
210 [Exodus 25:8]

For this, God has given us a special way to protect the house, and that is the commandment of *mezuzah*, about which our Sages, of blessed memory, say that the house is protected through it.

Furthermore, the protection encompasses the members of the household even when they are away from home, as the verse states, "God will guard your departure and your arrival, from this time, and forever."[211] As it is explained in Jewish holy books, the name of God that is written on the outside of the *mezuzah*, [*Sha-dai*,] is an acronym for the words that mean "the One who guards the doors of Israel."

We must also remember that all Jews are like one body and are united with each other. Therefore, the *mezuzah* is a Godly protection not only for the house and for everyone and everything in the house, but every kosher *mezuzah* placed in a doorway of some Jewish home strengthens the safety of all Jews, wherever they may be.

Moreover, since as mentioned above, every Jewish woman is the *akeret habayit*, and every Jewish daughter is a future *akeret habayit*, they have a special merit in the commandment of *mezuzah*. That is, one should strive to see that not only is there a kosher *mezuzah* in one's own home on every door which is obligated to have one, but also in the homes of their neighbors and acquaintances and in all Jewish homes.

STUDY QUESTIONS:

1. What is the first step one must take in strengthening his or her safety?

2. What kind of partnership do the Jews and God have to ensure the Jews' safety?

---

211 [Psalms 121:8, *Artscroll Tanach*, Mesorah Publications, Ltd., Brooklyn, New York, 2003]

3.   What about the Jewish home ensures that God will protect it?

4.   Which mitzvah gives special protection to the Jewish home?

5.   Does this mitzvah protect the members of the household only when they are at home, or also while they are away from home?

6.   How does one Jew's performance of this mitzvah help all Jews?

7.   What is the special obligation of the *akeret habayit* regarding placement of a mezuzah in every doorway that needs one?

Parashat Eikev

MAKING GOD'S PRESENCE
PERCEPTIBLE IN ALL ASPECTS OF LIFE

In *Parashat Eikev*, Moses continued his final speech to the Jewish nation. He spoke of the special qualities of the Land of Israel – the land which they would soon enter. Moses described it as "a land that the L-rd your God seeks out; the eyes of the L-rd, your God are always upon it, from the beginning of the year to year's end."[212]

In the following excerpt from a discourse, the Rebbe explains that the above-mentioned verse expresses the most significant feature of the Holy Land; the concept that God's presence is apparent in all aspects of life in the Land. By making God's presence apparent in all aspects of life, a person can bring some of the holiness of the Land of Israel into his/her own life. This is achieved by acting in a way that reflects the awareness that God is always watching.

Jewish women have a unique appreciation for the holiness of the Land of Israel, as we know from the story of the daughters of Tzelofchad.[213] Therefore, women have a special ability and responsibility to express in their own lives the central concept of the Land of Israel; that God's presence is apparent in all aspects of life. If a woman carries out this responsibility, she will influence the affairs of her home in a way that extends even beyond her home's boundaries.

---

212 Deuteronomy 11:12, *Artscroll Tanach,* Mesorah Publications, Ltd., Brooklyn, New York, 2003
213 The chapter on *Parashat Pinchas* (page 205) elaborates on this topic further.

The Rebbe writes:
Likkutei Sichot vol. 4, pp. 1329-1330

In the Torah portion of the week (*Parashat Pinchas*), we find the women's love for the Land of Israel, as shown in the story of the daughters of Tzelofchad.

We also find the precedence of the women over the men at the giving of the Torah and at the building of the *Mishkan*, as the verses state, "So shall you say to the House of Jacob and relate to the Children of Israel"[214] — "The men came with the women."[215]

These three events – the giving of the Torah, the construction of the *Mishkan*, and the entrance of the Jewish nation into the Land of Israel – form an interconnected series of events. The beginning of it all is the giving of the Torah, because the Torah was God's blueprint for the creation of the world and the laws of nature, as indicated by the statement, "He looked into the Torah and created the world."[216]

The endpoint is the entrance of the Jewish nation into the Land of Israel, which fulfills God's ultimate purpose in creating the world – to make a dwelling place for Himself in this lowest of all worlds. When the Jewish nation entered the Land of Israel, over which God's eyes are always watching, they began to be deeply involved in worldly matters[217] – particularly agricultural work and other mundane occupations. However, in order to fulfill God's purpose in creating the world, this effort of theirs to perform their worldly work had to be permeated with the Godliness that is invested in the Land through God's constant watchfulness.

The intermediary that enabled the holiness of the Torah to permeate the Land of Israel was the construction of the

---

214 [Exodus 19:3]
215 [Exodus 35:22]
216 [*Zohar*]
217 [While the Jews were in the desert, they lived on miracles. Their needs for food, clothing, and shelter were all provided in a miraculous manner.]

Mishkan – which was at once a physical object made of gold, silver, and copper, and at the same time contained a supernatural object, the Ark, which both did, and did not, occupy space.[218]

In all three topics, we find that the women had a special merit, to the extent that it was specifically through them that the men could be involved in these areas. As it is written in connection with the Giving of the Torah (the initiation of all these topics and the means for fulfillment of them), "So shall you say to the House of Jacob and relate to the Children of Israel." Through God's beginning, the Giving of the Torah, with the House of Jacob [the women], the Children of Israel [the men] received it also.

The lesson from this for Jewish women in every place and at all times is:

The whole idea of the Land of Israel, which "is a land that the L-rd your God seeks out; the eyes of the L-rd, your God are always upon it, from the beginning of the year to year's end," depends specifically on them. Through their love of the idea that God's eyes are always upon it, i.e., that Godliness should be perceptible in all areas of their life, they influence not only the conduct of their homes, but also the conduct of their husbands outside the home as well. Wherever the husband is, even when he is involved in his business and like matters, he will act in a manner that results from contemplation of the fact that God is standing over him...and watching him, "examining his kidneys and heart [i.e., his innermost thoughts] to determine whether he serves Him properly"[219] — God's eyes are *always* upon it.

---

218 [The Torah gives the dimensions of the Ark, the room in which it was housed, and the space between the Ark and the walls. It turns out that the total space between the Ark and the walls equals the width of the room, so that the Ark itself did not occupy any space.]

219 [*Likkutei Amarim — Tanya*, Rabbi Schneur Zalman of Liadi, Kehot Publication Society, Brooklyn, New York, Chapter 41.]

Through this conduct of bringing Godliness into all areas of life, actual blessings in material matters are increased. As the verse says, "I will fear no evil, for <u>You are with me</u>."[220] All the obstacles and hindrances are nullified — "I will fear no evil." Furthermore, God gives one's livelihood in a tranquil and generous manner — "beside tranquil waters He leads me...my cup overflows."[221] Expansion in spiritual matters results in expansion in material matters — in children, health, and livelihood in abundance.

STUDY QUESTIONS:

1.   What three major events culminated in the Jewish nation's entrance into the Land of Israel?

2.   What major change took place in their lives when they entered the Land of Israel?

3.   How does God relate to the Land of Israel differently than He relates to the other lands?

4.   What special role did the Jewish women play in the giving of the Torah?

5.   How can a woman emulate the holiness of the Land of Israel in her own home?

6.   What positive effects and rewards come from emulating the holiness of the Land of Israel in one's own home?

---

220 [Psalms 23:4]
221 [Psalms 23: 2, 5]

Parashat Re'ei

THE SPECIAL QUALITY
OF A WOMAN'S CHARITY

In *Parashat Re'ei* we find commandments regarding several types of charity. One is that a tithe from one's crops be set aside for poor people every third and sixth year of the *Shmitta* cycle. Another is that one must be generous in giving and lending money to a poor person. From these as well as other commandments, it is clear that giving charity is an important obligation in a Jew's life.

In the following excerpt, the Rebbe describes the special quality of charity given by women. He cites a story from the Gemara, in which a man gave charity to the poor in the form of monetary contributions, whereas his wife gave ready-to-eat food to those in need. When the husband and wife both prayed for rain, her prayer was answered first, since her type of charity was more immediately available to the poor person.

One's financial and spiritual contributions to one's own children are also considered charity. As in the above-mentioned story, the mother's spiritual contribution to the children is generally more directly available than the father's. Although the father usually hires a teacher for his children, the mother teaches them herself by supervising their conduct in daily life and making sure that they observe the commandments properly. Therefore, material blessings come to the family more quickly in her merit.

The Rebbe writes:
Likkutei Sichot vol. 2, pp. 580-581

The Gemara[222] relates a story of Abba Chilkiya and his wife, who both gave charity. When there was a need for rain, and both of them prayed, her prayer was accepted before her husband's.

The Gemara explains the reason: The charity that Abba Chilkiya gave to the poor people was in the form of money, which they could then use to buy food and their other necessities, whereas his wife, when a poor person would come, would give him food itself, not just something with which to buy food. Therefore, her prayer was accepted before his.

The Gemara says about someone who provides food and support for his young sons and daughters, that the verse, "...who performs righteousness (*tzedaka*[223]) in every time," [224] refers to him. That means that the idea of charity applies not only to strangers, but also to one's own children. This statement is not only a reference to material charity, but to spiritual charity as well, since educating one's children is indeed a form of charity.

Just as with charity in general — the man gives the poor person a prerequisite for something that he needs, and the woman gives him the food itself — the same applies to the spiritual charity, the education given to one's own children. The man, the father, gives the child the prerequisites, but the mother gives the child the spiritual food itself. That is, the father in most cases fulfills the commandment given to him, "You shall teach them thoroughly to your children," [225] not by

---

222 *Ketubot* 50a
223 [The word *tzedaka* can be translated as either 'righteousness' or 'charity.']
224 [Psalms 106:3, *Artscroll Tanach,* Mesorah Publications, Ltd., Brooklyn, New York, 2003]
225 [Deuteronomy 6:7, *Artscroll Tanach,* Mesorah Publications, Ltd., Brooklyn, New York, 2003]

learning with the child himself, but by hiring a teacher for him.

A story is told about the Alter Rebbe, according to which he called in a Chassid and said to him, "I have to fulfill the commandment of 'You shall teach them thoroughly to your children,' and you have to fulfill the commandment of providing food and support for your household. Let us make an exchange — I will pay you for your expenses, and you will learn with my Berel." He took him on as a teacher for his son, who would grow up to be the Mitteler Rebbe, the second Chabad Rebbe.

We find that when the father gives charity to the child, he does not give him the spiritual food itself, but rather the prerequisite for it — he gives money to the teacher, and the teacher learns with the child.

However, what the mother gives the child is the spiritual food itself. She must see that the child wears *tzitzit*,[226] washes *negel vasser*,[227] and says blessings, etc. That is because even though the child learns in a yeshiva or a *cheder*, it is possible that while the child is at home, he will lose everything that he absorbed when he was in yeshiva or *cheder*. Therefore, the mother must be attentive and guide him in proper conduct.

The rains of blessing for the whole house come more quickly in her merit. Therefore, the Torah calls the Jewish mother by the name *akeret habayit*, because she is the foundation of the House of Israel.

---

226 [*Tzitzit* refers to a four-cornered garment with fringes on each corner. The Torah commands that these fringes be worn on four-cornered garments, and they serve as a reminder to perform God's commandments.]

227 [*Negel vasser* is the ritual washing of hands that is done before the morning prayers.]

STUDY QUESTIONS:

1. Why was Abba Chilkiya's wife's request for rain answered before her husband's request?

2. What types of support that parents provide for their children qualify as charity?

3. What is the difference between a father's and a mother's "spiritual charity"?

4. What is the nature of a mother's spiritual charity toward her children?

5. In the context of the mother's spiritual charity, why is the mother called the *akeret habayit* – foundation of the home?

Parashat Shoftim

SENSITIVITY TO HOLINESS

In *Parashat Shoftim*, God instructs the Jewish people not to emulate the unholy practices of the nations that were living around them in the Land of Israel. In particular, God forbade the practice of witchcraft, which was often used by non-Jewish nations to find out what would happen in the future. Jews are not supposed to inquire about future events, but to trust in God and wholeheartedly accept whatever He sends their way. As the Torah says, "You shall be wholehearted with the L-rd, your God." [228] *Rashi* explains this verse to mean that one should follow God with perfect faith, without feeling a need to know what will happen. [229] Thus, a Jew must stay on the path of holiness – the path of trust in God – and avoid paths of unholiness.

In the following excerpt from a letter, the Rebbe explains that women have a God-given sensitivity to what is good and holy, as well as to what is unholy and must be avoided. Therefore, the women were the first ones to contribute toward the building of the *Mishkan*, but refused to participate in the building of the Golden Calf. Because of this special sensitivity, they have a responsibility to use their influence to guide their families, and the whole Jewish people, along the path of holiness.

---

228 Deuteronomy 18:13, *Artscroll Tanach,* Mesorah Publications, Ltd., Brooklyn, New York, 2003
229 *Rashi's* commentary on Deuteronomy 18:13

The Rebbe writes:
Likkutei Sichot vol. 6, pp. 366-367

Your undertaking occurs during the time of year when we read the Torah portions that tell about the building of the *Mishkan* — God's holy dwelling place — and about the part that the women played in it.

Certainly the content of these Torah portions will again call attention to and underscore the importance of the woman and daughter in all details of Jewish life — as tone-setters and guides.

As the Torah tells, the women were the first to contribute a portion toward building the holy dwelling place for God's Presence and they refused to take part in the Golden Calf, which was the opposite of holy.

A sensitive Jewish woman and daughter feels with an internal, God-given sense that which is holy and must be protected and that which is harmful and must be distanced from Jewish life.

In the present time, when good and evil, and light and darkness, are often confused for one another, it is more than ever a vital necessity that this internal, God-given sense that the Jewish woman and daughter have be expressed in day-to-day life.

Actually, this is the main task of the Organization of Chabad Women and Girls (N'shei uBnos Chabad): to bring out the Jewish woman's and daughter's internal sensitivity, and their feeling of responsibility for occupying their rightful place in the Jewish nation and as *akeret habayit*. In addition, their task is to constantly remember that in their hands, in large measure, lies the future of the Jewish nation.

STUDY QUESTIONS:

1.   What are two examples in the Torah of women's special degree of sensitivity to holiness?

2.   From where does this special sensitivity originate?

3.   Why is it more necessary now than ever before for the Jewish woman to make use of this sensitivity?

4.   What is the main objective of the Organization of Chabad Women and Girls?

5.   What is the far reaching effect of the conduct of Jewish women?

Parashat Ki Teitzei

MODEST CONDUCT BRINGS GOD'S PROTECTION

Parashat Ki Teitzei describes commandments that must be observed by the Jewish army in a time of war. These commandments apply to various aspects of the soldiers' lives, and help ensure that they will be in a state of purity, both physical and spiritual. In concluding this section, God says, "For the L-rd, your God walks in the midst of your camp to rescue you and to deliver your enemies before you; so your camp shall be holy, so that He will not see a shameful thing among you and turn away from behind you." [230]

The following excerpt is from an address of the Rebbe to a convention of N'shei uB'nos Chabad, the organization that encompasses all Lubavitch women and girls. In this discourse, the Rebbe mentions the above-mentioned verse in a much broader context than that of soldiers fighting in a war. He explains that when God sees that among the Jewish people, wherever they may be, there is no immodest conduct, He gives us victory over our enemies and grants us peace.

Although the Rebbe mentions this verse in connection with what was the uncertain situation in the Land of Israel when he delivered the discourse in 1970, it is more relevant than ever today. When the Jewish people act, dress, and speak in a modest manner, then we help to bring additional protection from God to the Holy Land and wherever it is needed.

---

230 Deuteronomy 23:15, *Artscroll Tanach*, Mesorah Publications, Ltd., Brooklyn, New York, 2003

The Rebbe writes:
Likkutei Sichot vol. 8, pp. 226-227

The Jews, even when they are dispersed, are one nation. Every one who is a member of the Jewish nation feels a connection and unity with every Jew, wherever he may be found. Certainly, this unity is felt to the greatest extent with Jews who live in the Holy Land, in the good and spacious Land, the Land of Israel. These Jews need a special blessing, and a special protection from God, to extricate them from the situation in which they presently find themselves.

The blessing from this week's Torah portion should be fulfilled: "You will dwell securely in your land." [231] The Jews should dwell safely in the Land of Israel, as well as every Jew, wherever he may be, in a manner of, "You will lie down, with none to frighten you." [232] Even when one lies down to go to sleep, he will not need a guard, because he is certain that "no one will frighten" him — not only will no one cause him harm, but they will not even do anything frightening. This Godly protection is due to the fact that "God is your Guardian" [233] at every moment. This guarding occurs at every moment, as the verse states, "He neither slumbers nor sleeps, the Guardian of Israel" (Psalms 121:4). The very idea of sleep is irrelevant with reference to God. Rather, God says to the Jews, "You will lie down and your sleep will be pleasant." [234] That is to say, "you can sleep peacefully, since I stand and protect you."

A factor that is necessary in order to have this Godly protection is the proper observance of modesty, as the verse says, [235] "for the L-rd your God walks in the midst of your camp" because "He will not see a shameful thing among

---

231 Leviticus 26:5
232 [Leviticus 26:6]
233 Psalms 121:5
234 Proverbs 3:24
235 Deuteronomy 23:15. The commentator Ibn Ezra explains the words "shameful thing" to refer to deed or speech.

you." When God sees that the Jewish people, wherever they are, have nothing immodest in their midst, then God goes among them — "to save you and to deliver your enemies before you." When this is the case, we do not even have to act militarily, since God Himself delivers "your enemies before you" — so that all of the Jews' enemies are destroyed and fall before the Jews. It is these very enemies that will be the ones to seek peace with the Jews.[236]

STUDY QUESTIONS:

1.   What connection does every Jew have with the Jews who live in the Holy Land?

2.   What special blessing from God do the Jews of the Holy Land need?

3.   What does the blessing "You will lie down with none to frighten you" mean in practical terms?

4.   What times of day does God guard the Jews?

5.   What behavior of the Jews evokes God's protection of them?

6.   To what extent will God protect the Jews if they behave in the proper way?

---

236 [This concept is illustrated in the verse] Proverbs 16:7

Parashat Ki Tavo

BEING HAPPY BRINGS BLESSINGS

Parashat Ki Tavo describes the blessings bestowed on the Jewish people if they observe the commandments properly. It also describes at length the curses that will befall them if the commandments are not observed as they should be. One transgression that is explicitly mentioned as a reason for the curses is a lack of appreciation of all the good things that God does for us. As the verse says, the curses would come upon the people "because you did not serve the L-rd your God amid gladness and goodness of heart, when everything was abundant." [237] From this negative statement, we may infer a corresponding positive statement – that serving God with joy brings blessings.

In the following excerpt from a letter, the Rebbe explains that the more trust in God one has, and the more joy with which one serves God, the more blessings will God give him. Furthermore, the mood in the home – the degree of happiness and gratitude to God that the family members feel – depends on the mood of the woman, the foundation of the home. She needs only to contemplate the kindness that God has done for her in the past to trust that He will continue to deal kindly with her in the future.

The Rebbe writes:
Likkutei Sichot vol. 14, p. 358

In reply to the news received from your husband, the Rabbi — may he live long and good years — about your

---

237 Deuteronomy 28:47, *Artscroll Tanach,* Mesorah Publications, Ltd., Brooklyn, New York, 2003

birthday, may it be God's will that the coming year should be a peaceful year, and a good and successful year such that the good is visible and apparent.

It is simple to understand that the greater one's trust is in God, the Creator and Governor of the world who watches over each and every individual with His Divine Providence, the more blessings one will be able to receive from God, and the greater is the measure of one's blessings and success. The teaching of our Torah, the Torah of life, is well known: A person must be happy and in a good mood, since all of the days, hours and moments of these days[238] are devoted to the service of the Creator. As the Torah states, [if the curses mentioned in *Parashat Ki Tavo* would come upon the people, it would be because they did not] "serve the L-rd your God amid gladness and goodness of heart."

This teaching is especially applicable to the woman, the *akeret habayit*, since it is apparent and perceptible that the mood in the home depends on the mood of the woman. Furthermore, one can only receive God's blessings if one is in a happy state of mind. Since we are commanded to do this [i.e., be in a happy state of mind], it is certainly feasible to do so. In particular, [an easy way to achieve a happy state of mind is to] contemplate — even for a short while — how kind God has been to you and your husband in the past. Certainly, He will continue to act kindly in the future.

As mentioned above, the means by which to receive God's blessing is a strong trust in God, and a genuine and true happiness. May it be God's will that this year God will fulfill, in a positive way, your wish to have children.

---

238 [This letter was written on the second of Nissan.]

STUDY QUESTIONS:

1.   What are two roles of God that make it reasonable to trust Him?

2.   What are two positive results from having trust in God?

3.   What negative effects could come about from not serving God with happiness?

4.   Upon which member of the family does the mood in the home depend?

5.   What is a good thought to contemplate to help oneself achieve a happy state of mind?

6.   What are the means by which to receive God's blessings?

Parashat Nitzavim

OBSERVANCE OF THE COMMANDMENTS
EVEN IN A FOREIGN LAND

This Torah portion explains that after the Jewish nation settles into the Land of Israel, they will become attracted to idol worship. God will then punish them by sending them away from their land into exile, where they will ultimately repent and return to God.

In modern times, many Jews emigrated from the deeply rooted Jewish communities of Europe and Russia (the so-called Old Country) and came to America to rebuild their lives and communities. The spiritual problem posed by American life is that various influences may cause Jews to compromise their observance of the commandments. As America is a "modern" place, there is a feeling that it is not necessary to observe the commandments so scrupulously.

In the following excerpt, the Rebbe writes how in America, as much as in the Old Country, we must wholeheartedly observe the commandments and connect ourselves to God. In particular, the Rebbe stresses the need for women to observe the laws of modesty as diligently in America as they or their ancestors did in the Old Country.

The Rebbe writes:
Likkutei Sichot vol. 6, p. 364

As soon as the Previous Rebbe came to America, in the year 1940, when he revealed his God-given assignment in this land to transform America into a place of Torah and fear of God, people would ask him, "Isn't this America, a place that is different from the Old Country?" To this, the Rebbe would answer emphatically:

"America is no different! America is no exception in the area of Torah and the commandments!"

This statement has a special significance for Jewish women. In certain respects, it has even more significance for them than it does for men. In general, women have an inclination to follow the latest fashions, and it is not uncommon for the fashion to have a negative effect on the observance of the laws of modesty. Jewish women must realize that the same Torah and commandments and the same principle of, "The entire honor of a Jewish daughter is within,"[239] that were valid in the Old Country, are also valid in America.

Throughout the ages, Jewish women have had a tradition of being strong in their dedication to the observance of commandments. In Biblical times, the women were the first ones to help build the *Mishkan* for the whole Jewish nation. In more recent times, they established a holy sanctuary within their own homes in the Old Country, making their households a place about which God can say, "I shall dwell among them,"[240] a home within which God could be present, so to speak. This same tradition is as valid here in America as it was in the past in the Old Country on the other side of the ocean.

STUDY QUESTIONS:

1. What question did people in America often ask the Previous Rebbe soon after he arrived in America?

2. What did the Previous Rebbe mean by the statement, "America is no different"?

---

239 [Psalms 45:14]
240 [Exodus 25:8]

3.   What particular challenge do Jewish women face in maintaining their observance of Jewish laws?

4.   What concept should Jewish women keep in mind in order to successfully meet this challenge?

5.   What positive examples of women successfully meeting the challenge does the Rebbe mention?

Parashat Vayeilech

ASSEMBLING ONE'S PERSONAL CAPABILITIES
FOR THE SERVICE OF GOD

In this Torah portion the commandment of *Hakhel* is stated: every seven years, all Jewish men, women, and children are obligated to come to the *Beit Hamikdash* to listen to the king read certain Torah passages. The purpose of this gathering is to motivate the nation to fear God and observe all of His commandments.

This stress of *Hakhel* — of working on one's fear of God and observance of commandments — is something that applies to each Jew's life today as well. In a letter to the graduating class of Bais Rivkah High School, the Rebbe explains the special role of women in observance of the commandment of *Hakhel*. He then shows how the Jewish women of today must fulfill a comparable role and exert a positive influence on their environment.

The Rebbe writes:
Likkutei Sichot vol. 19, p. 546

In general, the idea of *Hakhel* was to <u>assemble</u> all Jews – men, women, and children – with the purpose of strengthening the nation's fear of God and observance of the commandments in daily life.

A person is called a "small world," a world in miniature, with a whole array of spiritual and physical capabilities. Therefore, in one's personal life, the idea of *Hakhel* must remind us of the importance of a continual mobilization of all of one's capabilities toward the same objective – to strengthen the fear of God and observance of the commandments in one's personal day-to-day life.

It is worth making note of the fact that because even the youngest children had to attend *Hakhel*, the women (the mothers and older sisters) had a special task to bring them and care for them. This further underscores the special duty and merit of Jewish daughters in the strengthening and dissemination of Torah and the commandments in a pure and holy way.

May God grant that the concept of *Hakhel*, in connection with your graduation, as mentioned earlier, should constantly accompany you on your path in life, and you should be a source of good influence and encouragement to all those around you.

STUDY QUESTIONS:

1. Who was supposed to attend the *Hakhel* event?

2. How was the *Hakhel* event supposed to affect those who attended it?

3. How can a person today emulate the *Hakhel* event in his/her own life?

4. What special role did the women play in the *Hakhel* event?

5. What can women of today do emulate the special role that women played in the *Hakhel* event?

Parashat Ha'azinu

In *Parashat Ha'azinu*, Moses delivers a prophetic, poetic speech to the Jewish people. This speech contains basic principles to guide them through their future as a nation. He begins by describing the greatness of God and the many kind things He has done and will do for the Jews, such as bestowing great material wealth upon them. However, their response will not be one of gratitude, but of rebellion. As the verse says, "Yeshurun became fat and kicked. You became fat, you became thick, you became corpulent — and deserted God its Maker."[241] This reaction of the Jews reflects an improper attitude, which they must be careful to avoid.

In the following excerpt, the Rebbe describes the correct mindset one must have toward the acquisition and possession of material wealth. He points out that the woman of the home, the *akeret habayit*, is the one who must instill within her family the proper attitudes regarding material wealth. She should convince her husband to truly believe that wealth comes from God's blessing, and that if he trusts in God, then a minimal effort on his part will enable him to receive God's full blessing. In addition, she should instill within her children the proper Torah attitudes, including that one should not aspire to acquire the same material possessions others have.

---

241 Deuteronomy 32:15, *Artscroll Tanach*, Mesorah Publications, Ltd., Brooklyn, New York, 2003

The Rebbe writes:
Likkutei Sichot vol. 2, pp. 527-528

When one does not seek luxury and knows that blessing comes from God and that one need only make a vessel [to contain the blessing] and rely on God, Who is omnipotent, then even when one makes a small vessel, God fills it with abundant success and great wealth – actual material wealth.

One must not pursue wealth and luxury. When one refrains from pursuing them because he knows that the main thing is spirituality, and that he needs only enough material wealth for what is needed to fulfill the commandments of the Torah, then God gives from His full and broad hand abundant wealth — even material wealth.

Furthermore, adherence to this idea of not pursuing luxury and superfluous matters depends on the *akeret habayit*.

She should help her husband understand that the main thing is the spiritual nature of the home, not the material nature. Therefore, he need not intently pursue his livelihood day and night in such a way that he would not have any time to learn Torah and devote himself to general matters. He also need not pursue earning more and more money for purchasing superfluous items.

She should also explain to him that intently pursuing a livelihood cannot help him at all, because a person's sustenance is allotted to him during the time between Rosh Hashana and Yom Kippur. The amount of money he will earn is designated then, and he will certainly not receive more than what was decided upon for him. Furthermore, he can receive what was allotted to him by making even a small vessel, without many trials and tribulations.

What is the point of pursuing a livelihood with great exertion, when one must then ensure not only that God blesses him with money, but that He will also protect him from harm? It is easier to rely on God, realizing that God's blessing is what makes one wealthy, and then one is safeguarded in all areas.

When the husband hears these ideas from his wife, then even if luxury has some importance to him, these ideas have an effect on him and make him ashamed to reveal this desire to his wife. Then, he does not feel influenced to have nice furniture and nicer curtains on the windows than the neighbor has.

He stops wasting energy and money in order to accumulate possessions, thereby accumulating worries,[242] but rather, he begins to say, "I have everything" (everything in Heaven and earth). He unifies materiality with spirituality, makes his home a holy abode for God, and stops pursuing his livelihood day and night. Instead, he makes a vessel for God's blessing, designates time for learning Torah, and relies on God.

Then, God's blessing will make him wealthy, and not only is the money not spent on medical treatments, etc., but also he has a generous income. He earns enough money with this generous income to give charity with an open hand and a joyful heart, and he and his wife and children are happy.

This same idea is applicable to the education of children — sons and daughters — i.e., that the goal to which one should devote oneself is to educate one's children according to the path of Torah and its commandments, to see to it that the children grow up to be *Chassidim*, God fearing, and devoted to learning Torah. This brings eternal happiness to the children as well as the parents.

However, when one devotes oneself to adorning the child with expensive clothing in order that the child should wear nicer clothing than the neighbor's child, the happiness that this brings can last a day, a week, a month, or a year. Afterwards, when the child grows up, he realizes that his

---

242 *Pirkei Avot* 2:7

parents neglected to give him true happiness through which he would be happy his whole life.

This too depends on the Jewish woman, because she is the *akeret habayit*. Therefore, it is specifically she who is able to establish the conduct of the children's education, and also the conduct of the whole household, so that it will be a happy home spiritually, and therefore also happy materially.

STUDY QUESTIONS:

1.   What is the best way to achieve success and material wealth?

2.   What can a wife tell her husband to convince him not to pursue wealth and luxury?

3.   When is a person's income determined?

4.   How would a husband react if his wife explains to him the true source of wealth?

5.   What are some of the blessings God would give if a person has the proper attitude toward material wealth?

6.   What can parents do to help their children have the proper attitude toward material wealth?

7.   What special capabilities does the *akeret habayit* have in affecting the conduct of the household?

Parashat Vezot Habracha

EDUCATION OF YOUNG CHILDREN

In *Parashat Vezot Habracha*, Moses gave his final speech to the Jewish people, in which he blessed each tribe. In his introduction he made the statement, "The Torah that Moses commanded us is the heritage of the Congregation of Jacob."[243] This statement is a fundamental principle in Judaism, and therefore it is the first verse of Torah that a father should teach his child once his child learns to speak.[244]

In the following excerpt from a letter to a women's convention, the Rebbe mentions this requirement of the father. He contrasts it with the mother's influence on the education of her child, which, by contrast, begins immediately, right after birth. Even later, when the child has already begun to speak, her close relationship to the child allows her to have a greater influence on him. God gives the mother the strength to fulfill this vital role in the education and upbringing of her children, and helps her do so with joy and Chassidic warmth.

The Rebbe writes:
Likkutei Sichot vol. 13, p. 149

As has been mentioned many times, our Sages, of blessed memory, emphasize the fact that when God gave the Torah, He first approached the women ("So you shall say to the House of Jacob") and only afterward the men ("and relate to the Children of Israel").[245] Similarly, in the education of

---

243 Deuteronomy 33:4, *Artscroll Tanach*, Mesorah Publications, Ltd., Brooklyn, New York, 2003
244 *Shulchan Aruch, Yoreh Deah* 245:5
245 [Exodus 19:3]

children, the mother comes first, since the education of a child in the first years after birth is exclusively in her hands. Only later, when the child begins to speak, does the father teach him, "The Torah that Moses commanded us..."

However, even in the later years, the mother has a greater influence on the children, young and old, due to her special close and loving relationship. We also see this in connection with the commandment of honoring one's father and mother, about which the Torah states, "Every man, your mother and father shall you revere"[246]— to have respect for one's mother and father, with emphasis on the mother, who is mentioned first. That is because, taking into account that the relationship between the mother and her children is permeated mainly with love, the Torah especially cautions regarding fear (i.e., respect) toward the mother, as *Rashi* explains on the verse.

God has given the Jewish wife and mother a special responsibility — and together with that a special privilege — with regard to Torah in general, and specifically with regard to education of children. Therefore, it is a certainty that He has given to them, as well as to the Jewish daughters who are preparing themselves for the most important role as *akeret habayit*, special capabilities to carry out their God-given mission to the fullest extent, with joy and with Chassidic warmth and light.

STUDY QUESTIONS:

1.   From what point in a Jewish child's life does his mother begin educating him?

2.   From what point in a Jewish child's life does his father begin educating him?

---

246 [Leviticus 19:3]

3. When the child grows older, which parent has a stronger influence on the child?

4. What can we learn from the commandment to revere one's parents regarding which parent has a more loving relationship with the child?

5. How does God help Jewish women to exert a proper influence on their children?

Appendix

Below is a table that shows the chapter and verse with which each *parsha* begins and ends.

Parsha	**Beginning Chapter and Verse**	**Ending Chapter and Verse**
Beraishit	Genesis 1:1	Genesis 6:8
Noach	Genesis 6:9	Genesis 11:32
Lech Lecha	Genesis 12:1	Genesis 17:27
Vayeira	Genesis 18:1	Genesis 22:24
Chayei Sarah	Genesis 23:1	Genesis 25:18
Toldot	Genesis 25:19	Genesis 28:9
Vayeitzei	Genesis 28:10	Genesis 32:3
Vayishlach	Genesis 32:4	Genesis 36:43
Vayeishev	Genesis 37:1	Genesis 40:23
Miketz	Genesis 41:1	Genesis 44:17
Vayigash	Genesis 44:18	Genesis 47:27
Vayechi	Genesis 47:28	Genesis 50:26
Shemot	Exodus 1:1	Exodus 6:1
Va'eira	Exodus 6:2	Exodus 9:35
Bo	Exodus 10:1	Exodus 13:16
Beshalach	Exodus 13:17	Exodus 17:16
Yitro	Exodus 18:1	Exodus 20:23
Mishpatim	Exodus 21:1	Exodus 24:18
Terumah	Exodus 25:1	Exodus 27:19
Tetzaveh	Exodus 27:20	Exodus 30:10
Ki Tisa	Exodus 30:11	Exodus 34:35
Vayakhel	Exodus 35:1	Exodus 38:20
Pekudei	Exodus 38:21	Exodus 40:38
Vayikra	Leviticus 1:1	Leviticus 5:26

Tzav	Leviticus 6:1	Leviticus 8:36
Shemini	Leviticus 9:1	Leviticus 11:47
Tazria	Leviticus 12:1	Leviticus 13:59
Metzora	Leviticus 14:1	Leviticus 15:33
Acharei Mot	Leviticus 16:1	Leviticus 18:30
Kedoshim	Leviticus 19:1	Leviticus 20:27
Emor	Leviticus 21:1	Leviticus 24:23
Behar	Leviticus 25:1	Leviticus 26:2
Bechukotai	Leviticus 26:3	Leviticus 27:34
Bamidbar	Numbers 1:1	Numbers 4:20
Naso	Numbers 4:21	Numbers 7:89
Beha'alotecha	Numbers 8:1	Numbers 12:16
Shlach	Numbers 13:1	Numbers 15:41
Korach	Numbers 16:1	Numbers 18:32
Chukat	Numbers 19:1	Numbers 22:1
Balak	Numbers 22:2	Numbers 25:9
Pinchas	Numbers 25:10	Numbers 30:1
Matot	Numbers 30:2	Numbers 32:42
Mas'ei	Numbers 33:1	Numbers 36:13
Devarim	Deuteronomy 1:1	Deuteronomy 3:22
Vaetchanan	Deuteronomy 3:23	Deuteronomy 7:11
Eikev	Deuteronomy 7:12	Deuteronomy 11:25
Re'ei	Deuteronomy 11:26	Deuteronomy 16:17
Shoftim	Deuteronomy 16:18	Deuteronomy 21:9
Ki Teitzei	Deuteronomy 21:10	Deuteronomy 25:19
Ki Tavo	Deuteronomy 26:1	Deuteronomy 29:8
Nitzavim	Deuteronomy 29:9	Deuteronomy 30:20
Vayeilech	Deuteronomy 31:1	Deuteronomy 31:30
Ha'azinu	Deuteronomy 32:1	Deuteronomy 32:52
Vezot Habracha	Deuteronomy 33:1	Deuteronomy 34:12

Glossary

Akeret habayit — The wife/mother, who is the spiritual foundation of the Jewish home.

Alter Rebbe — Rabbi Schneur Zalman of Liadi, author of *Tanya* and the *Shulchan Aruch HaRav*; founder of Chabad *Chassidut*.

Beit Hamikdash — The Holy Temple in Jerusalem.

Bar / Bat Mitzvah – A term used for the time at which a Jewish boy / girl reaches the age of 13 / 12. This is the age at which a child becomes obligated to obey the commandments

Chassid (*-im*, plural) — A follower of the Chassidic movement.

Chassidut — The teachings or philosophy of the Chassidic movement. *Chassidut* is a user-friendly approach that provides deeper insight into God and His creations.

Cheder (pl. *chadarim*) — A Jewish elementary school, in which the main focus is on teaching and learning Torah.

Chinuch — Jewish education according to Torah standards.

Gemara — Rabbinic discussion on the *Mishna* and other topics the *Mishna* raises or suggests. It constitutes the major part of the *Talmud*.

Gilgul — Return of a soul to a new body.

Kashrut — The Jewish dietary laws.

Kohen (pl. kohanim) – A Jewish man who is of direct patrilineal descent from Aaron, the first *Kohen Gadol*. In the days of the Holy Temple, the *kohanim* performed the ritual services in the Holy Temple.

Kohen Gadol — The High Priest who served in the Holy Temple.

Manna — The food that God miraculously provided for the Jewish people while they traveled through the desert from Egypt to the Land of Israel, as described in the Torah (Exodus 16)

Mashiach — Messiah, the leader of the Jewish people who will usher in the complete redemption.

Menorah — The candelabrum in the Holy Temple, which held seven candles

Midrash (-im, pl.) — Collections of Scriptural interpretations by rabbis of the Talmudic era.

Mishkan — The Tabernacle, a portable sanctuary, built by the Jewish people in the desert, in which God's presence was manifest.

Mishnah – First major written compliation of the *Oral Torah* by Rabbi Yehuda HaNasi around 220 C.E.

Mitzvah (pl. Mitzvot) – A commandment of God as expressed in the Torah

Parasha(*t*) — Weekly Torah portion (of)

Pirkei de Rabbi Eliezer – A *Midrashic* commentary on the Bible ascribed to Rabbi Eliezer ben Hyrcanus (80 – 118 C.E.)

Rashi – Acronym for Rabbi Shlomo Yitzchaki (1040 – 1105), who was the author of comprehensive commentaries on the Torah and the Talmud that are the most influential and widely studied of all Jewish commentaries.

Sefirah — The period of time between the holidays of Pesach and Shavuot.

Shmitta — The Sabbatical year, which occurs once every seven years. During this time, agricultural work is forbidden to Jews living in the Land of Israel.

Shulchan Aruch — The most popular and widely-referenced code of Jewish law, authored by Rabbi Yosef Karo.

Shulchan Aruch HaRav – A codification of Jewish Law by Rabbi Shneur Zalman of Liadi, the first Rebbe in the Lubavitch dynasty.

Talmud — A record of Rabbinic discussions pertaining to Jewish law, customs and history. It is the first written compendium of the *Oral Torah*.

Tanya – A primary book on Chassidic philosophy authored by Rabbi Shneur Zalman of Liadi, the first Rebbe in the Lubavitch dynasty.

Tefillin — A set of two leather cases containing Torah passages. It is strapped onto the arm and head by Jewish men during weekday morning prayers.

Torah, Oral — The *Oral Torah* refers to the teachings that God gave to Moses at Mount Sinai, which were not written down immediately, but rather transmitted orally from one generation to the next until they were ultimately written down in the *Talmud* and in many other later works.

Torah, Written — The *Written Torah* refers to the Bible. It is contrasted with the *Oral Torah*.

Tosafot – A set of medieval commentaries on the Talmud.

Tzemach Tzedek – The third Rebbe in the Lubavitch dynasty. Also known as Rabbi Menachem Mendel.

Tzniut — Modesty in conduct and attire.

Yeshiva — A religious school dedicated to the learning of Torah.

Yom Tov — A Jewish festival.

Zohar — A fundamental book of Kabbalah.

Index

Abraham 27, 28, 29, 30, 31, 32, 33, 45, 52, 117

Adam 17, 18, 19, 21

Akeret Habayit 43, 44, 45, 53, 61, 62, 72, 73, 74, 79, 102, 112, 121, 122, 133, 134, 139, 147, 168, 177, 185, 186, 192, 193, 203, 216, 223, 224, 225, 233, 236, 244, 253, 254, 256, 258, 263

Army of God 175

Asenath 61, 62

beauty 37, 38, 111, 112, 113, 129, 130, 197

challah 69

charity 94, 130, 131, 231, 232, 233, 255

conquering 53, 66

danger 27, 29, 125

descent of generations 11, 137, 151, 152, 247–48

desert 85, 94, 98, 116, 125, 126, 176, 177, 187, 195, 197, 206, 209, 211, 219, 228, 264

Dinah 47, 48, 49, 50, 51, 52

education of children 33, 34, 61, 78, 79, 82, 85, 86, 87, 89, 90, 94, 96, 102, 109, 113, 162, 163, 164, 186, 232, 255, 256, 257, 258

Egypt 61, 65, 66, 67, 68, 69, 71, 77, 81, 85, 86, 89, 91, 92, 97, 116, 122, 164, 175, 177, 188, 198, 207

embarrassment 55, 56, 179, 180, 181

emotions 56, 57, 58, 59, 95, 106, 117, 156, 216, 243, 244

enthusiasm 17, 19, 121, 220

Eve 17, 18, 19, 21

Evil Inclination 18

exile 59, 66, 68, 71, 74, 75, 78, 82, 91, 94, 143, 146, 175, 188, 198, 247

family purity 69, 112, 139, 140, 151, 152, 153

fear of God 77, 79, 165, 247, 251

God's presence 17, 109, 111, 121, 227, 264

hair covering 34, 179

helping another Jew 159, 160

holiness 33, 34, 72, 74, 92, 112, 125, 129, 133, 145, 153, 167, 168, 171, 172, 187, 189, 212, 227, 235

influence 33, 43, 44, 48, 51, 53, 65, 66, 78, 95, 106, 138, 140, 148, 151, 157, 191, 192, 220, 227, 229, 235, 251, 252, 257, 258

intellect 56, 57, 58

Isaac 33, 38, 43, 45, 117

Israel, Land of 30, 85, 167, 176, 177, 187, 188, 189, 205, 206, 209, 210, 211, 212, 219, 220, 227, 228, 229, 235, 239, 240, 247, 264

Jacob 43, 45, 47, 48, 49, 50, 51, 52, 53, 58, 61, 68, 71, 72, 73, 74, 101, 102, 117, 228, 229, 257

Jerusalem 98, 162, 163, 165

Joseph 61, 68, 71, 74

joy 62, 89, 90, 91, 92, 95, 96, 97, 98, 106, 162, 243, 257, 258

Judah 55, 56

kashrut 69, 112, 137, 139, 140

Kohen 74, 111, 133, 134, 146, 179, 183, 185, 192, 263

Kohen Gadol 33, 35, 155, 156, 157

Leah 46, 47, 48, 49, 50, 51, 52, 117

love of fellow Jew 159, 185, 192

Machpelah, Cave of 71, 72, 73, 74

marriage 147, 148, 215–16

material necessities, lack of 62, 168

mezuzah 223, 225

Miriam 77, 78, 79, 89, 90, 91, 92, 95, 96, 97, 177, 195, 196, 198, 212

modesty 34, 50, 53, 110, 163, 164, 171, 172, 202, 203, 240, 247, 248, 265

Moses 18, 65, 77, 78, 81, 86, 89, 90, 91, 95, 96, 97, 101, 102, 111, 115, 121, 122, 125, 161, 175, 187, 191, 192, 195, 196, 198, 205, 206, 207, 215, 219, 227, 253, 257, 258, 265

Previous Rebbe 78, 82, 90, 106, 247

purifying the world 21, 66, 69

Rachel 46, 49, 71, 72, 73, 74, 117

Rebbetzin Chaya Mushka 81

Rebecca 43, 117

redemption 58, 59, 66, 68, 69, 75, 77, 78, 81, 82, 85, 91, 126, 135, 143, 146, 163, 164, 264

reward 71, 72, 91, 116, 117, 160, 165, 172, 179, 180

sacrifice, ritual (korban) 134

Sanctuary 98, 109, 111, 121, 122, 125, 126, 129, 133, 134, 155, 172, 188, 204, 228, 235, 236, 248, 264

Sarah 33, 37, 39, 40, 117

security 223, 240

self-sacrifice 55, 56, 59, 73, 74, 78

Shabbat candles 69, 105, 106, 112, 143, 144, 145, 146, 147, 148, 183, 185

Shlomit bat Divri 161

Shmitta 167, 168, 231, 264

sociability 161

success 48, 53, 79, 87, 102, 110, 126, 139, 147, 159, 216, 224, 244, 254

Tamar 55, 56

Torah, giving of 17, 18, 44, 85, 86, 94, 96, 101, 102, 176, 188, 228, 229

Torah, learning 73, 102, 130, 131, 132, 157, 168, 171, 220, 254, 255

trust in God 62, 68, 115, 117, 215, 216, 219, 235, 243, 244

Tzelofchad, daughters of 188, 205, 206, 207, 215, 227, 228

vows 209, 210, 211, 212, 213

wealth, material 94, 131, 180, 231, 253, 254, 255

Yocheved 65, 68, 77, 78, 79

Made in the USA
Columbia, SC
12 September 2020